Q-Art is run by a team of students and graduates and supported by
a panel of active members from the Q-Art community. Our aim
is to break down the barriers to and between various models of art
education and make the workings of the contemporary art world
more transparent. Our focal activity is an open crit, which we run
monthly across various UK art colleges and gallery spaces for anyone
to attend or present work in. We also run workshops and produce
publications. Other publications by Q-Art include:

11 Course Leaders: 20 Questions
– A collection of interviews with 11 London BA Fine Art course leaders
(Ed.1 2011). (Ed.2. 2013)
ISBN: 978-0-9564355-1-4

Art Crits: 20 Questions
– Featuring interviews with UK fine art staff on the topic of the crit.
(2013). ISBN: 978-0-9564355-2-1

Interviews gathered between October 2007 and September 2008.
First published in 2008 by Q-Art London.
Foreword and Introduction written in 2008.
Second edition published 2009.
Third edition published 2013.
ISBN 978-0-9564355-0-7

Second and third edition designed by Jens Dan Johansen
www.jensdanjohansen.com

Proof-reading: Fiona Flynn

'Q-Art' is the trading name of Q-Art London Community
Interest Company. Company No. 8587499

12 GALLERISTS:
20 QUESTIONS

CONTENTS

ACKNOWLEDGEMENTS

With thanks also to:

Aidan Sheridan

Evelyn Wilson

Jason Grant

Julie Taylor

Katie Yates

Mike Metelits

The Q-Art Team

Q-Art's current, previous and future
participants and supporters

FOREWORD

By Sarah Rowles, Director, Q-Art

Viewing art in the market place I became increasingly confused with what was being presented to me as contemporary art. At the outset, before interning at a number of galleries both in the East and the West End of London, I presumed that this was because I didn't understand contemporary art[1], presuming also that the market place and the galleries shared the same codes as the art institution; that all gallerists, art educational institutions and buyers had a collective language with which to evaluate works. I saw what I felt were poor pieces being bought for thousands of pounds – I thought they must be understanding something I did not.

The gallery is an interesting and unsettling interstice between the institution of the art school and what is the final resting home for precious few artworks, the institution of the museum. I wondered what happens in this middle ground, what codes are in place, and how an area with seemingly so little transparent critical criteria, can legitimately come to evaluate art. It is a place where in some cases art can be both bought and sold by those without art backgrounds.

As a student, my incentive in carrying out these interviews was to try and gain as much understanding of this area as possible. It is an arena that from the outside seems that because of a dominance of networking, money and trends, the hard-working artist has little control over their future artistic success.

I took a series of simple questions to the twelve gallerists, hoping to gain some real insight and knowledge of this area, so that it might help myself and others navigate a path through this notoriously mystified system.

This project owes a lot to all of the gallerists who took part and I thank them for their generosity, both with their time and answers.

---

1   In the interviews 'contemporary art' refers to work that is recognised and endorsed, or in the process of being endorsed by leading art markets, writers and institutions. The concept of endorsement is central to how a work is accepted into the art markets and institutions. London, like Berlin and New York, is a global centre for such endorsement and much of the contemporary art world activity.

INTRODUCTION

By Nina Danino

These interviews, comprised of 20 questions addressed to selected London gallerists, give an insight into how different gallery spaces survive, the artists that the gallerists promote and how galleries represent artists – what they do for them and how the art makes the transition from art school to marketplace. Behind the international visibility of chosen contemporary art lie questions such as how is new art evaluated by the gallery system once it exits art schools and by whom? What is endorsement? We get a sketched map of how art travels into institutional acceptance and come to appear in our museums.

The conversations are frank about the determining role of finance, the rents, the cost of running the business and inevitably broach the concealed subject of the buyers – a jealously guarded source of funding necessary for the continuation of the production of art for most artists who show in the gallery system. Who are the buyers? Why do they buy art? What do they do with it once they have it – especially if it is a large work? How are prices decided? How does what the buyers want affect what is produced in art? The so-called 'contemporary art fair look' and the need to sell, prompts concerns over a lack of support in the market for more ephemeral media such as video, installation and performance.

A mix of both privately and publicly funded galleries from the East End and West End in London are represented. The gallerists occupy a variety of niche markets and social spaces and have different histories as well as different personal approaches and goals for the art that they are interested in and have different social motivations for opening and running an art gallery.

Many of the gallerists lead us through a brief history of the gallery scene in London over the last two decades. Some galleries have weathered the transition of the evolving economic climates. Some have witnessed how the rise and fall in both collector audiences and Arts Council funding have had a profound effect on the way they operate. Robin Klassnik is one of the few gallerists who since opening up in 1979 as the first artist-run gallery in England, has remained revenue funded by the Arts Council. Others who began as non-profit, publicly funded spaces, have with the huge increase in the demand for contemporary art, the arrival of Zoo (2004), Frieze (2003) and the Arts Council's decision to work more closely with the private sector, been forced to run their gallery as a business. The artist-run spaces mushroom with different ideas for survival; the latest one being to offer artists shares in the (business) space. The interviews give glimpses into the travails and ups and downs of galleries as business ventures, the current state of the art market and the pressures they face in order to survive.

The interviews are a testament to how the rise of the market has overshadowed the evaluation of artwork away from art criticism, powerful art critics and intellectual self-criticism by artists, to the control of the gallery. Outside of art education, having a gallery and 'endorsement' are increasingly important in promoting the art of a new artist.

How does this market evaluation sit against the criticality by which art is valorised within art education? To what extent is the aim of a gallery-life for art after art school relevant to art students in an environment free from these market constraints? How do these two spaces educational and post educational affect each other? Does fashion or marketability influence what is produced in art school? Robin Klassnik raises the question of whether young artists run the risk of not learning their craft and that "many do not even know what they're doing at art school now". I would say that students understand the world of contemporary art, at least from the outside and some have a keen awareness of the system, what they are doing and how to achieve it.

Once outside of the critical framework within art education, art seems to circulate exclusively in the colder semantic field of money, business and brands and artists are not encouraged by this system to present or discuss their work critically. I have wondered why it is acceptable to the bright minds of art students and contemporary artists that once outside of the art institution they should present themselves in role of the inarticulate, naïve or uncritical artist.

The interviews address the exhibition of art after art school and remind us of the subjectivity behind 'endorsement'. They raise the question of value judgements and how taste making is in the hands of if not a few individuals, and then of a market system, which is also called 'the art world'.

The gallerists talk about their passion for art as well their business side. This recent hyper marketability of art has undoubtedly created an excitement around art. That is why there is a hugely enhanced social and public awareness of the culture of art; of going to see it and buying it, which tends to dominate the view of art and what it can do for cultural prestige and social mobility. These interviews talk to some of the people who are involved in it and open up questions about it to new artists who want to get a foothold in these systems. They try to open up for outsiders how things work in the art world, hopefully contributing to the demystification of the gallery system.

Nina Danino,
Filmmaker, Artist and Lecturer in Fine Art (Department of Art, Goldsmiths)

MOTINTERNATIONAL

Founded as an artist run initiative by Chris Hammond in 2002. In 2006 MOT became MOT-INTERNATIONAL and has since represented emerging and established international artists though a commercial dealership. It also runs a commercial curatorial practice.

Can you tell me a bit about how the gallery started?
Originally I rented my studio in Limehouse in the nineties. I got frustrated with making and not exhibiting and with putting exhibitions on in other places, as these were expensive. I curated a few warehouse shows of other artists before deciding that I'd make my studio into an exhibition space. I then had the economy to show my work and a space in which to invite other artists along to show their work at the same time. It fitted with what I was thinking about and I became more interested in exhibition strategies, which would now be termed curating, and less interested in the making.

Would you have a gallery anywhere other than London?
No, it'd be quite pointless. London is where it's all happening really, even on a global level. London, New York, Berlin, it doesn't really get much better than those three cities. But you never know; other places have interesting scenes too, like LA.

Why are you located here in Bethnal Green?
People collect together. I chose this because there was a cluster here already and it was an emerging scene. On a Sunday people can see many different small shows and it's better than going to a museum in many ways. I mean

you came here and already in this block alone there are three galleries. And if you go across the road there's Vyner Street.

Do you ever associate with other gallerists?
Yes we associate and we get together at art fairs, especially if you're in another country. Originally when I first started here I did a show where I showed the artists who ran artists run spaces and called it *Space Men.*

Have there always been lots of galleries in the East End or has this been a fairly recent phenomenon?
Since around the late nineties there were some. One of the first people who came here was Anthony Wilkinson and he's since built his own gallery on Vyner Street. Then Approach moved in the nineties. There have also been lots of people in and out of the same spaces.

So MOT was originally a non-profit space?
Yes until this year, 2007. We changed into a hybrid space, which is sort of a new thing really. We used to be project by project fundraised for every single exhibition in the same way that an institution would be, except we didn't have core funding. A lot of the exhibitions MOT used to do in the first few years were funded by the Arts Council or The Elephant Trust and we'd raise money to do the show.

What is a hybrid space?
We now represent artists in the traditional gallery dealership sense but also maintain a programme of independent projects that we continue to go to funding bodies for. Either that or we use the money we make from the dealership and go to art fairs and sell work from our gallery artists to put back into the programme.

MOT is also well known for being a curatorial practice. We've worked with lots of independent curators and those curators independently have also worked with exhibitions at MOT. They raise a project and we work together to get a project done. That's now a commercial curatorial practice so if people want me or one of the other independent curators associated with MOT to put on an exhibition somewhere they'll have to create a budget and our fees will come out of that.

Now that you are a commercial dealership do you have a body of artists that you represent and does representation dictate that you can show only them?
I show them but I also do independent exhibitions. But now that is less so. We used to put on eight exhibitions a year and eight of those exhibitions would be independent. Now only one or two might be. It depends on the economics of the moment. You can also exchange artists to achieve an international programme.

How does that work?
One can show people from other galleries in say the US or Europe and then they show your artists. That's how you get the international programme.

How do you decide which artists you are going to represent?
Years of experience, I've been curating for a long time now.

Do they come to you or do you go after them?
I go after them. People do come to me but they tend not to be very good.

But if you're going to them are they not already represented?
Some are, but maybe not in the UK. We've got a good reputation and people want to buy into that history. The art world is very small so most of the better artists have been around sometime. You all know them or have even shown them. I mean I've exhibited a lot of people I represent in our independent programme so I know their work or I made a relationship from that.

Well if this is the case and you go after artists who are already out there, how are any new artists to make headway?
Well, what a lot of people do is peer-represent. One person in a year group

will be perhaps more into doing a gallery and then represent artists that were in their generation. That's what a lot of people started out like.

Do you like the work of the artists you represent?
Yes, of course.

Would any gallerist take a work on if they don't like it but because they think it will sell?
You'll have to ask them. You can cynically say it looks to be that way but it's hard to know. Some gallerists are strictly business people and it doesn't really matter if they like it or not. But a lot of gallerists were artists – you'd be amazed at how many went to art school.

What does representation involve?
We're like an agent for the artist. You are doing more for them than just selling their work, you're promoting their career, you're trying to get them into exhibitions at the Tate, you're trying to push them into exhibitions all around the world. You also try to get their work into collections that are considered to be good. It's not just anybody who comes off the street you sell it to who wants to buy the artists' works. The big galleries will only want to sell to well-known collections.

Why?
That's looking after their artists' careers. That way they become more established.

So most sell it to collectors who have good collections?
Yes. I mean a good collector will have lots of historically important artists in their collection.

And could a collector then donate a work to a museum?
Or lend it, yes. If an artist's career is expanding and they start to be sought out to be in museum exhibitions then curators will ask to borrow work.

Invariably, the collector will want to lend that work to a good museum because one, it makes their collection worth more and two, that's part of what a collector collects for. They like being involved in that whole art world. They get invited to the big dinners and they see their work up in a museum. So for them it's like a badge of honour, because it's their piece. The artist enjoys being shown at the Tate but the collector is the same – "well I chose that work, it's mine" and everybody else is looking at it and thinking "wow I wish I owned that".

Other collectors give to museums because they're generous and also it's a tax write off. If you have a big collection that's worth lots of money you definitely want to keep that in a public museum rather than in your house.

Where do collectors store their collections?
Lots of very big collectors have offshore storage or they keep them in storage units run by shipping companies like Momart art handlers. Big galleries have got their own warehouses where they store work.

Is most of the art wanted by museums tied up in private collections?
Yes. It's the curator's job to secure loans and to borrow works.

Are galleries less likely to sell to those buyers who are looking to make a quick profit?
If a gallery thinks the collector's going to sell it on the secondary market they won't sell to them because that kills the value of the work.

Do auction houses cater for the secondary market?
Yes. They are there for collectors to sell their work.

Why would a collector want to sell work?
They might want to change part of their collection and they make money if they sell it. They're not supposed to do that right away but they may do in the future. Even big collectors put a portion of their collection on the market, they might want to buy a new young artist and think well you

know if I sell this old Gerhard Richter then I can buy a whole body of work by this young up and coming artist. That's quite normal.

Is the only way for a piece to enter a museum via a gallery or collector?
Mainly, but museums do have their own purse. Though it's very small. There are patrons and people who buy for museums as well as charities like Outset who buy works to donate to museums. The Arts Council also buys certain amounts of work by new artists, as does the government.

Is a gallerist the same as a dealer?
Similar I suppose. Most gallerists are dealers but you can also be a dealer without a gallery. There are dealers who source works for their clients who have trusted them to buy for their collection. So the dealer will come to a gallery and buy work. They will add their commission to it as well so the collectors pay two different people.

Do any collectors open up galleries?
Yes most of the major collectors build their own galleries in order to show their collections.

How is a work first given a price?
By the gallery and the artist together.

But it can increase, so who decides the increase?
The collector or whoever's got it. If a collector buys it then they can decide how much they want to sell it for. This will be whatever the market will take.

Do you notice any current trends, debates going on in art?
There are probably always trends; you have to look out for them yourself. People buy contemporary art now more so than ever before. How does a collector judge whether a work is good if it's by a new artist?

They go to recognised places and they trust the press to write about artists. It's all validated by reviews, exhibitions in museums and the reputation of the gallery they show with.

Is it possible that one piece might be no better critically than another but sell for more money if it is by a bigger artist or a more powerful gallery?
Yes. And if you're a top gallery artist then you're going to sell more than any artist with a younger gallery. But then people go to younger galleries to see what's going on and what's going to be new. There are lots of things going on in a dealer's mind as to why they choose the artist or not.

Do you think it's possible that what dealers or collectors buy could ever influence what kind of art artists are making?
I hope not. I think the tutors on degree courses would be shocked if students wanted to make work that sold.

Where do you find your collectors?
At art fairs or if they come to the gallery because you are showing an artist who they have heard of.

Do many people buy at art fairs?
It depends which art fairs you go to. The fairs in London, New York, Basel and Miami are always busy and there are usually several fairs running at the same time.

So they must know what they want. How do you know which works you're going to take along?
You look at what you think will go well together. You obviously want to curate a good stand and this depends on who you're pushing at the time. You might want to have a big drive about one artist and you might want a bunch of museum directors to see a whole body of their work. Also collectors start collecting a certain artist.

What do you think of art fairs?
It's not the best place to view art, but it is good for collectors and curators who want to see many works and discover new artists in a short space of time, in one place. Exhibitions such as the Venice Biennale are perhaps better in terms of providing a context.

Documenta, Venice, are the works there on sale?
No, but they will probably be available through each of the artists' galleries.

UNION

UNION was founded by Jari Juhani Lager in September 2003. It operates across two galleries in both South and East London.

How old is Union and has it always been in this location?
It is four years old now and yes, it has always been here.

You also have another gallery, why?
Yes correct, in Teesdale Street in the East End. I started there with a project space called VTO many years ago. After eight years I decided that I didn't want to continue to that space anymore but I liked the location. I then got this building and it seemed like a good idea to keep this and have a smaller space for younger artists or those who work on a smaller scale. The two shows here and there co-ordinate quite well.

You said the other gallery was originally a project space, what does this mean?
That was how it started. A project space is a non-commercial space. It's the idea that you work a bit more experimentally with artists who do not necessarily want to be represented. It's like a curated exhibition, so the actual financial connection tends to be different from here.

So would those works in a project space be for sale?
They are for sale for the period when they are exhibiting.

So that was what inspired you to set up here?
Union was created here, before it didn't exist. To create a solid identity now both galleries are called Union.

So now both Union galleries are commercial?
Yes, but the space over there is still considered more like a project space because there's no reception.

Have you always been in London?
Yes.

Would you have a gallery anywhere else? Why?
No. Well for the future I was thinking of Berlin but everybody is opening a gallery in Berlin now so I find that it's less exciting because of that.

Berlin is supposed to be cheaper than London isn't it?
Yes. In London you have many artists who live and work here. There are in Berlin as well but it's less of a profession. More people move there and that is why there are so many galleries in Berlin now, there are three hundred.

As far as art is concerned do you think London is the place to be in the UK?
London has advantages. But relatively few galleries come to London because they find it too expensive.

Though surely most of the money is in London? Most of the collectors come to London, I presume?
Yes, but that's not what people understand. They are more worried about spending than earning. And it's true, we spend a lot more money than we would if we were anywhere else but we also make more money.

How did you first manage to set up, if it was so expensive?
Luck. It's very difficult to survive I think.

Do you see a difference between the galleries located in the East and those in the West?
I think the East End started off with the idea that it was cheaper to find a place. It was smaller and allowed for more experimental spaces but these

then turned into commercial spaces to make more money. They all booked themselves into Vyner Street, which is becoming a bit of a gallery ghetto. They support each other in that so many visitors run through and obviously collectors go there. We don't have collectors swarming in here every single day and so we are at a bit of a disadvantage in that sense. But we have a nicer space than many other galleries. So maybe we get fewer visitors but those who come and see us find out that we have really good shows and that gets talked about.

You do still get collectors here though?
Yes, though maybe less. That's why we do more art fairs and we communicate a lot through email. And our website is designed well, more targeted towards people.

Do you only show the works of artists that you represent or do you borrow works?
Some works I borrow.

How do you decide which artists you will represent?
That always depends on how good they are. It has to do a lot with commercial success as well or how much you believe in them. It's a difficult process.

Do you usually approach them?
I try to, yes. Before, when I did the project space, it was a different sort of network that I was following. It was like I meet him and then through him I meet him and projects would come out of discussion. Then that was okay because there was no commercial involvement in the process.

So now you are commercial how do you find your artists?
Now I look around and if I see someone I like I may have to collaborate with other galleries because the artist may already be represented. But this might work because maybe this artist already has an established market but hasn't shown in London yet. London becomes an important city in this case where you can actually present other people's artists.

Do you represent artists?
No, we show them. I have to be careful with the word representation because I don't really know what it means myself anymore. The whole art world was very clear before the Internet because then, if you needed to contact the artist you would go to the gallery who's fixed to the artist. Nowadays all you need is a telephone or email address and people can talk directly with the artist or with some other strange dealer or agent. It's a bit...

... Clouded?
Yes, clouded. Now someone who likes a piece and buys it can suddenly become a dealer as well. Collectors are becoming dealers. It has become quite messy.

Do you always take artists whose work you like?
Yes, I mean that's...

Do you think anyone does the opposite just because they think they can sell it?
There are always people who do that.

How much commission do you take?
Generally it's fifty-fifty but it changes because costs are shared. It maybe sixty-forty, seventy-thirty and it depends on the scale of the project. I mean we're now in the middle of a big commission in Mexico, which is a half a million-dollar installation, and there it's impossible to have fifty per cent, you just wouldn't be able to sell it. So most of the money is anchored into production costs with some fee for the artist and some fee for the gallerist.

Are collectors expecting it to have commission added?
Many expect fifty percent and that is why they try to work discounts. But in situations like this you say well look, the calculation is very different, this is a technical structure and most of the money is tied into the actual making of it. Most collectors understand that. When it's a painting

though, prices get a bit funny because they want them to be validated by the auction houses.

Aren't auction houses for older artists?
They can decide what they want to sell.

The pieces in there would be pieces that collectors have sold on?
Exactly.

How are price increases decided?
Take Damien Hirst. The last price decides the next one, so his prices are changing according to the market. It means that again and again you have to find a new type of collector as the prices go up. You're reaching out to some very different types of people and you obviously have to make a different effort. I mean the effort behind Hirst's operation is probably incredible in terms of PR, there's a whole team behind it. You just don't do that by yourself. You have to contact hundreds of journals everyday and there are probably about ten people all doing PR, but that's what keeps his popularity and his visibility all over the world. People will always want to come from all over the planet for an interview, that's how it is.

Is there such a thing as good art? Is there such a thing as standards? And how does a collector know when a work is going to be valuable or not?
It's what they call 'the eye'.

It's odd though to think that one work might sell for far more than another based on subjectivity?
Well, careers change for artists as well. One minute they're doing one thing and it's great, then because they change their style – or even because they don't – they disappear or drop, change or no change.

Do you have your own list of collectors?
Yes.

Are there trends you can sense people buying at the moment or does it vary from person to person?
It varies. Asian art, Indian art, Chinese art, it sometimes goes in regions.

Are you less likely to sell a work to a collector who you suspect is more interested in a profit than the art?
Well this is an issue because if you don't sell at market price it is a risk. If a collector comes in and wants a body of work for thirty percent discount for example then you sort of wonder what he is doing. Maybe he has a very large space or collection. But if a month later it ends up in auction then it is obviously frustrating because they sell work for market price and make more profit than us as a gallery.

How does going to auction affect the artist's value?
It's very risky because you can change the whole price structure for an artist.

Do you sell more at an art fair than at any other time?
At an art fair you can show much of your programme and people can also approach you much later. If you're not there then people ask why not and you lose a degree of visibility. People notice that and so you get a lot quieter. Though it's very expensive I find.

How much was the rent at Zoo Art Fair?
Eight thousand pounds, though some smaller ones are four thousand. I had a lot of work so I needed to invest in a larger space. If you only have a small stand you can't show as much.

How do you decide which works to take to a fair?
We just take what's in our programme. We try to do something beautiful. We rotated the works. I don't like to hang artists on the same wall. It's my style to present it more elegantly and I had a lot of artists who wanted to show. It was good, yet sometimes we missed some people who wanted to see a particular artist.

Had you shown at Zoo before?
Since the beginning I was asked to participate. The application is tougher now I believe.

Is it the ultimate goal to get work into museums?
We have almost all of our artists in museums and recently one of our Korean artists got a solo pavilion at the Venice Biennale – you can't get higher than that! For me that was a fantastic experience to know that an artist I picked to show before anyone else showed him went to Venice. Though I don't represent him fully and the only disadvantage is that once they reach that level that's all they want and you hope that they don't forget you.

HOXTON SQUARE GALLERY

Richard Maddalena set up Hoxton Square Gallery in 2005. The gallery which is open to all artists to exhibit resides in both Hoxton Square and virtually on the website. I met Richard at *Art in the Dark*, one of the events put on by the gallery as part of Time Out's *First Thursdays*.

Do you do different events for every First Thursday?
Yes that's how it has worked out. Potentially I might repeat something though, like *Art For Nothing* where we invited artists to give away their work to the public free of charge. I thought we'd take money out of the equation and just look at art directly.

It's a nice idea. Did people take the work?
Oh yes, they were quite hesitant at first though.

Well because nothing comes for free anymore, does it?
I think it does come for free and there is art being given away for free. It's just that the media has taken the focus off of that and works are being judged by how much they sell for rather than the weight of what's actually in them. So one of the ideas of art for nothing was to shift the focus back onto the art, rather than the money.

There's a lot of mystique surrounding the art world, I'm trying to uncover it a little...
I'd go for it. If you get hesitant answers it's a sign that people are more frightened of you than you are of them. This is because there's a certain amount

of mystique building that goes on, especially when it's linked to sales. I mean when you're justifying the latest version of blank canvases and the large selling price, you have to create a mystique.

Many will try to give you the impression that they know everything and are on this higher plane or have the giant overview, but they haven't, they're struggling like everybody else. There will be people with large amounts of knowledge out there yes, but no one person has a full picture.

Remember, fear makes people rude. If you're asking somebody who's prime interest is to show a sense of power they'll go frosty on you. The simple questions are the most frightening for people in that position. Somebody coming along asking questions can be like throwing a spanner in the works, they'll try and make you look like you've got the wrong answers.

Do you think there is a way into the art world without the aid of an institution?
It's a boundary, isn't it.

You must have noticed that the attachment of an institutional 'brand' lends a certain level of endorsement?
Yes that's often how it is.

(An artist comes along saying he wants to perform)

Do you need to speak to him?
No I don't make contracts with artists, everybody is individually responsible. So if an artist is amazingly successful they're not successful because of me. Also if an artist goes psychotic that's not my responsibility either.

What was your idea behind setting this up, the virtual space and the performances?
It's the idea that an artist exhibiting should be as easy as setting up a game of Frisbee. It shouldn't be seen as a long grind in order to get your work out there. It's trying to inspire confidence out of showing the work; to use Joseph Beuys' quote: "everyone is an artist". That should be so. I wanted to open

it up and stop that sense of mystique that people have about the art world. I'm not trying to sandbag it, I'm not trying to be deliberately simple, but I am trying to be less precious. I have it in a central area of London but at the same time I'm not dominated by money. It costs me about £16 a year for the website and I have the entire square. Of course everyone else has the square too but I'm setting an example. So if you come to me and say "Give me your gallery" I'll say "It's yours here for you anyway".

So can artists just come to you and say "I want to do this thing"?
Yes, use it, yes. People say "Do you want to look at my work?" and I say "No, it's okay". I don't mean that as an insult, I just don't want to make judgements.

I might see something that I think is bad selling for thousands of pounds and something that I see as really quite good not selling for much. Why does that happen? Is it just a question of who has the most power behind their opinion?
It's almost like water running on the ground. If you give the ground a poke in that direction the ground will open up and the rest of the water will follow. It's by somebody's say-so, plus people are trying to get a hand on investment so it's tied in with money too. Successful investment involves working out which way the market is going and that's a separate dynamic altogether really. I think if you pinpointed that one you could probably go and work for Ladbrokes or something. Once the artist is established in the money side of things it doesn't matter what they make. Their work is still going to sell at the highest price because of a name, the artwork is no longer being judged.

Did you go to art school?
I did. I started working in newspapers for Fleet Street but I didn't like where I was going and they were paying me bad money. So I applied for a Foundation. But then I was on my way to Morocco, didn't get there and wound up in Madrid making paintings. I made my living selling those alongside more unconventional art performance. Now I'm selling fewer paintings and experimenting and I've got a bit of money backing me. But artists making

deals is not where I put my energy. I'm not against selling I just don't want to put my energy there. I'm just keeping money out of it.

So you don't take commission if the artists sell at one of your events?
No.

MATT'S GALLERY

Director Robin Klassnik founded Matt's Gallery in 1979. It is a publicly funded gallery and was the first artist run space in England.

Can you tell me about your gallery?
The gallery is twenty-nine years old and it started September 16th 1979.

(Front bell rings – it is a private day)

We've always had a bell at the gallery, ever since the beginning and it has been quite important. In 1979 this would not have been a common occurrence as it was the first artist-run gallery in England. When I started there were no others and no competition either.

Where did it begin?
It started off in my studio on Martello Street, London Fields, within a stone's throw of Vyner Street, and it didn't get endorsed. People thought 'He's an artist, why is he opening up a gallery? We're going to have herds of people traipsing through the studios...' We should have been so lucky.

And so it started. You had to ring this bell. It was a long way, it would take me three minutes to come down the fire escape, through the studio complex and there you would be met. Quite often I think people might have already left by the time I got there.

So you changed premises?
In 1990 we moved to Copperfield Road, Mile End, where we sit today. It's a much more luxurious premises and much bigger but philosophically the

concept of Matt's has never changed. I have always run it and it is now a publicly funded gallery.

There aren't that many publicly funded galleries now...
You must remember that in 1979 there was no market. There was no 'art fair'. Frieze is a recent phenomenon; it's only four years old. A lot of galleries who are opening up now are opening up to be commercial, and perhaps that is because there is no alternative for them.

Where do you get your funding?
My funding comes from the Arts Council and always has done. I believe in public funding. You have other publicly funded galleries who started within five or six years, I think the Chisenhale was the first and then the Showroom. But the big difference between those publicly funded galleries and mine is that they can have different people running them and they have been a stepping-stone for curators or directors to bigger and better things. But Matt's has not. The only stepping-stone has been for me and I've not yet reached the top. I'm still only half- way up the ladder.

There are so many galleries opening now...
It's different today. There was no such thing as clusters, clusters are a new thing. There are new ghettos of these galleries and they're all striving to make a living. But there is an audience for this. The audience for art has just got enormous, partly through Frieze and partly the Tate Modern. Nick Serota really has made art a sexy thing you know.

Do you think that all the visitors who go to Tate Modern are really engaging with the art?
No. But do people who go to Vyner Street engage with the art? They go, they look, but they might get caught, they might get trapped. And I think that's the beauty of Tate Modern. You don't necessarily have to know about art but you have to get them into the art gallery in the first place, you have to trap them. Once they're in they might get interested. But no they won't

all be interested. But anyone who goes to any art gallery must have some liking or hoping to find some kind of experience. They wouldn't just go there to stay out of the rain.

So do you believe that art should be accessible to everyone?
I think art should be accessible to everyone. I'm not necessarily saying that the art I put on here should come down to the lowest common denominator, I don't agree with that at all. I think art should be made as the artist wishes it to be made, however difficult it is.

In order to get money from the Arts Council do you have to meet certain criteria?
You have to fill out forms and it's got more complicated as the years have gone on, mainly because there are more people applying for it. When I originally got Arts Council funding I got two hundred and fifty pounds to put on a show. But I am a revenue-funded client, which means I get money annually and it is renewable every three years. It's not for life my funding, it might stop this year, for instance, as our contract with the Arts Council comes to an end in March. We've survived because of the quality of the art we've shown.

Why will there be cuts?
They have got very little money and there are so many people applying. They are taking a decision to fund fewer better, rather than just fund little bits. I think it's quite an admirable way to go.

You mentioned the clusters that have emerged. Do you think galleries benefit from that?
It draws more visitors in but I don't know whether drawing more visitors in is necessarily...

So do you think the quality gets poorer?
I think the quality is a lot poorer everywhere you go, but when you get fifteen exhibitions at once there's a lot of choice. You can walk in and walk

out. The philosophy of our gallery is that I don't really want people to just walk in and walk out. Some of the work is difficult but if you spend time within the confines of the art gallery it might just grow on you.

That goes back to one of your original questions about making art accessible. I think very difficult art can become accessible and you can get new people to enjoy contemporary art but they do need time. I put a show on here by Melanie Counsell and if you knew nothing about art it might have been difficult to take in. There was basically an empty room with a false ceiling. You could have walked in and out again… but I think there's more chance of doing that when you're in a street with lots of galleries.

Whereas if someone has come all the way out here they're going to want to spend more time in the gallery…
The idea of the trek has always been important to me. I don't think people trek as much as they used to. I have a big audience but I don't think it's as big as it could be because I think people start at Bethnal Green and have Matt's Gallery down on the agenda but might not come because they got tired. I think to some degree I am losing out because of where the gallery is located.

If you're a non-profit space can you sell works?
From time to time, but I don't call it selling. That's something that's never given me great satisfaction, though I have some of the most important artists living in the United Kingdom. For example Mike Nelson, who I've worked with since 1993, ever since he was a student… It's more important to me that I started working with Mike and am still working with Mike. Matt's Gallery is where he can take risks, where he made *Trading Station* and the show he's just finished making, which was nominated for the 2007 Turner Prize. I don't think he would have made that if it weren't for Matt's Gallery, where he knows he can take a chance and make something different to what he is getting known for.

Another artist that has worked with us since 1990 is Willie Doherty. We have sold Willie's work to the Tate. We do sell works to the Tate every three years and when it happens it's like Christmas. What I enjoy is to work with the artist and for them to take a chance. Even if the work fails I think that's quite important.

Are works made here?
All works are commissioned for the space; they relate to it either physically or psychologically. Nine times out of ten works have been made for this space. It doesn't mean they cannot be shown elsewhere; they can, but not as successfully. They can move but there will be a different kind of work when that happens.

Should I presume you've never had a stand at an art fair?
Never. There is some pressure from artists who think perhaps we should. Some of the artists I show like Willie Doherty are represented at art fairs by other galleries. We have teamed up with other galleries and some artists are now jointly represented.

What does the representation of an artist involve?
I think it varies from place to place. It used to mean something different. I think the whole art world has changed with the invention of email. Some artists now deal with their own affairs and there is no need for the gallery. They used to rely on the gallery because the gallery had a fax machine and secretarial back up and that was part of representation – doing his or her paperwork and answering questions. I think now it means going to art fairs and taking something to art fairs.

Where do you find new artists?
I've met many as students, by visiting them in their studios or at college.

What do you think about the large prices being fetched for art today?
It doesn't concern me really. Do you mean someone like Peter Doig or like Damien Hirst? Hirst's exhibition at White Cube, Hoxton Square, was fantastic – I loved it. I think he is a truly interesting artist: an artist and a

showman who knows how to manipulate everything he comes into contact with. I think the whole thing about his skull and the fifty million was the artist drawing attention to the nonsense about inflated prices in art.

Why are some works valued over others?
It's a matter of taste.

Would you be anywhere other than London?
It would be very difficult. I could only be somewhere other than London if I had private money. Then I could do what I do and we could still make the art. It might not have as large a public following… you'd either have to bus them in from London or not be worried about only two people seeing your exhibition.

And I do think the artist needs a public – I think it's unfair for him or her to make things in isolation.
How about if it were in another city? I know someone who studies art in Nottingham and they think that London and the rest of the UK are like two separate worlds when it comes to art. You should study in London or else you don't get much of a look in.

I went to a London art school and graduated in 1968. I think you can still get a decent education elsewhere but you have to make a trip to London from time to time to see what's happening, and I don't think that's a bad thing. Sometimes I think people from Sheffield know more about what's happening in London than those in New Cross. Sometimes you don't see things on your own doorstep and I don't think students in London see as much art as they should. They seem lazy.

Is it possible to spot any themes or trends in today's contemporary art? Can you see the direction it's going in?
I can't actually. The glib answer would be that they all want to be celebrities but that's not really true. I can't see where it's going but I think it's definitely getting less and less intellectual. I think everyone now actually believes that

when they hit art school they're going to be an artist in their first year and that they should be having an exhibition.

I'm not convinced it's the best thing in the world for young students to be exhibiting art. I think there's a risk that you don't learn your craft. I think there is a language to be learned or why bother going to art school in the first place? I'm not sure if a lot of artists know what they're doing at art school now.

Is it possible to spot standards?
Yes.

STUDIO 1.1

Studio 1.1 is an artist run space.
Here I am in conversation with Michael Keenan
and Keran James.

*Can you tell me a bit about what it means to be an artist-run gallery and how
it differs to other galleries?*
K: We know what it's like to be an artist. Lots of gallerists do of course, it's
how they started, but in time they leave it behind them and there becomes
a them-and-us thing. Studio 1.1 started out with six of us. We supported
the gallery financially and could do what we liked. However, because
we were all artists and all had our own practice, in the end most people
weren't willing to give that up. Gradually over the years it whittled itself
down to the two of us, but we still feel on that side of the fence. Running
a gallery for me has meant restricting my practice a lot, but I've been able
to persuade myself, as in any case a broadly conceptual artist, that my
practice has subsumed into running the gallery.

M: All galleries are different of course, even artist-run ones. As far as I
can see we're a bit more reckless than most. We don't like to say no to artists, even when it comes to knocking down the occasional wall, or fitting a
completely different set of lights.

What do you show?
M: We share a lot of opinions and tastes and pretty much agree on what
we're going to present. The main criterion is seriousness of work – work
that excites us and we want to bring to people's attention. There's certainly
no style or category of work that we would or wouldn't show. It's being
able to agree on that that makes it worthwhile.

K: We don't want a brand or a narrowly defined identity; the gallery
doesn't have to strive to be fashionable.

So you show quite a range?
K: Definitely. I'd like to be perverse and show something totally incomprehensible, though it doesn't have to be shocking. Or pick something most people wouldn't show in a gallery – even something that fails, shooting ourselves in the foot. Occasionally what we show even corresponds to the mainstream! It's good that people can't predict what we might show next.

So are you a commercial gallery?
K: We're not against selling and we need to sell a certain amount to survive. We don't have any other income to rely on, such as renting out studio spaces for example. It's important after all for the artist that we sell and it's frustrating when we don't. What we'd really like to do is expand the parameters of "commercial" so that we could sell so-called non-commercial work, on an on-going basis. I think that the art market as a whole is just too timid to step outside that idea of what is commercial.

M: What makes us not commercial I suppose is that we really have a different set of skills, not the right contacts and most importantly a different set of aims. We're not against selling but it's not why we're here. Of course, refusing to brand ourselves plays a big part. People don't think "Oh I know what I want and I can find it at Studio1.1". We're receptive to experimentation. And we hope for visitors who share that feeling.

K: We'd never be commercial in the conventional way. I'd like to think that if it ever became "We'll show him or her because they'll sell even though we don't like the work" we'd give up.

M: But it's good to try and find a balance.

K: Yes, we do try. Once we put together what we felt was a very well balanced and effective show in a set of offices in a loosely art-related environment. It was work that we felt was challenging but quite accessible. They hated it. But the show stayed up for three months and after that time a lot of the staff had become quite attached to some of it and had revised their opinions. The senior management on the other hand – that's a different part of the story.

M: We always thought that if we ran a gallery we'd be part of the art world, but as the years go by we discover we're completely outside of it. We don't fit in anywhere. Which I suppose can be a good thing sometimes.

Do you think there are galleries that take works on because they would sell even though they may not like the work?
K: Yes definitely. Quite often that's the only conclusion you can draw. Liking art doesn't necessarily come into the equation. It's a product they know how to handle, how to generate the buzz.

M: I'm not sure that it matters. You certainly won't find anyone being cynical and saying "Oh art's just another business". They're all 'passionate' about the art they sell but I'm sorry, you go from gallery to gallery and you think "Who the **** could be passionate about that?!"

Though I can see how one could be passionate about the actual business of selling, making deals, creating that buzz and finding the art that you can shift.

Are standards in art obvious or is it people's own opinions that elevate works?
K: I've always thought I have not wanted to prescribe what is and isn't art. All my life I thought absolutely anything can be, it's vital to have no boundaries. But the more and more I see things, I think not only wouldn't I show that – I don't actually think it's art. Or rather it's not about deciding what can be art but maybe who is or isn't an artist – and there are plenty of the latter around who are very successful.

I see nothing that is challenging me in a way that I want to be challenged, even like Matisse or Poussin still do. There's nothing going on in the mainstream that remotely challenges me or that I think I should be taking that seriously. And I want desperately to take art seriously.

M: In mid-nineteenth century France the most famous and successful artist was a painter called Meissonnier. His career overlapped with Manet's.

How do you think value gets attributed to such works?
K: Well who is attributing the value? I think fashion is what makes it. You can almost see things before they happen and you shake your head. If you go to Frieze you can see that what the next big thing is supposed to be has been decided upon. And there's a lot of money making sure that it works.

Are critical acclaim and monetary value linked?
K: They'd like to be but no, not really. The critics might play a small part in establishing a reputation, but after that there's nothing they can do. They can't destroy it as much bigger forces have taken over. Jonathan Jones of the *Guardian* is an important critical voice, and he's not afraid to be contrary.

M: But if his reviews had any impact on monetary value most of the YBAs would be selling the *Big Issue*.

K: It seems these days there's an awful lot of entertainment around but maybe there always has been. Something pretty and apparently meaningful, that appeals both to mainstream critics and hedge-fund managers. Lightly dressed women around an Arabic fountain by Lord Leighton for example would have its equivalent now with Cornelia Parker's exploded shed – I can't bring myself to call it *Cold Dark Matter*.

I'm tempted to go back and say "pretty and apparently meaningless" because I think that's where we are these days.

M: There is a very low-level category of lotto-type art where you can buy something for one or two thousand pounds and it's basically rubbish but it doesn't matter because there will be a replacement to excite you next year. For serious collectors with serious money this means as little as buying a lottery ticket, which is what it is. If it catches on fantastic, if not, it's not too bad.

The trouble is that a lot of the appeal at the moment is art's disposability. In the long run that is quite depressing because it looks like a slippery slope. There are people who are just beginning to make names and their work would generally be classed as conceptual but the concept has shrunk away to the size of a dried pea. All that remains is something that will be taken up and then something else that will be taken up. This will work for a while. Nowadays consumer goods are disposable so why not art as well? The fact that it is supposedly cutting edge is sufficient in itself; it doesn't matter what it looks like or what it might mean or do. Or what if anything it does to you. One can think "Oh I've got the next best thing".

K: If that's what you want then there's always the next big thing and then the next, next big thing. So it's an addiction that's encouraged. It's capitalism, consumerism. That survives and there's nothing much we can do about it except not be part of it.

M: It's very difficult for artists to come to terms with this. Most artists for example have a fixed idea of their monetary value and forget to take account of the fact that it has only got a value if someone wants to buy it. That's where the value comes from in anybody's case in the end.

Who do you think that the preferred audience is for a gallery?
M: Different galleries have different goals. Some galleries happily let you wander in off of the street and look at Picasso's or whatever. Others, you feel, roll their eyes as they press the buzzer to let you in. And there are a few with just a tiny brass plaque and no windows and no signs and they are pleasant enough once you get in but it's clear their preferred audience isn't time-wasters. In our case we like people to come and see the work, as many as possible, which is why we normally have the door open.

K: The other day someone came in and I said "hello" and he turned around to me and said "I'm not a buyer'".

What did you think of Zoo Art Fair?
K: The first year we put on a very beautiful show, a few pieces in this pure white space, really thoughtful. But the fair ran more like a car boot sale and we were totally unprepared to have people say "Oh I like that but do you have it in blue?" The next year we piled everything up but everyone else went for a restrained stand and looked down their noses at us. It can be depressing submitting to the pressure and the hard-nosed summings-up: "Who is this?" "Where did they study?" "Have they shown abroad?"

The best one of all is "How old is this artist?" and as happened to us, if you say seventy they then walk away because they are literally only interested in the future market or in other words, profit. But of course we still want to be in it – it confers a kind of recognition after all. Though we've never done anything more than cover our costs.

So do a lot of collectors go to seek out profit?
M: Oh completely, yes, and you can't blame them.

K: But the thing is you know they're going to get it wrong unless what's invested is not just the money but also the promotion that goes with it. You could go as far as saying that the really sensible collectors go to a buzzy gallery and say "Okay I'll have one from every show you have this year, I don't care what it is". Because a gallery's reputation these days is the safest bet you'll find.

M: I went around the fair without much enjoying looking at most of the art on show. So I started thinking, what would I buy if I had the money? And if I had had any, I'd still have had it when I left. Then I thought "What would I show if I wanted to make money?" and there was lots of that.

K: When Zoo first started it was supposed to be cutting edge young galleries and apart from the surprise of the car boot sale thing I was also surprised – Where is the cutting edge? Where is the challenging work? It seemed to be quite commercial in a way that we weren't expecting and over the years it has got more and more commercial. The first year the Kitsch level seemed much higher and was quite refreshingly silly, but now... or maybe now I'm just used to it. The thing behind it is there are just so many artists around looking for things to make art out of.

Do you think there should be some filtering system then to stop anything and everything getting through?
K: Well I never thought I'd say that until quite recently but yes. It seems to

be filtering the wrong way. It actually seems to me to be filtering out serious work, the real engaging and challenging work. At the art fairs you're supposed to be attracted to 'neo', which is okay, but none of the stuff is ever anything else.

M: I think that what we do but most galleries don't is take risks. Perversely because we're not commercial we've got nothing to lose. If the gallery closes – that's it – we've done what we can. We're there for our artists, to see what they make next, regardless of whether they sell and without having to say yes they tick these boxes and conforming to some fashion-led idea of what will sell.

Do you think it's possible to spot trends?
K: It is itself a cliché but there are so many one liners and these sadly are the successful ones. A trend is grabbing at straws and taking everyone with you. By definition you don't hear about the market's misses.

M: I think it's quite difficult. For collectors I think it's virtually impossible to see what the next best thing will be. If you are a commercial gallery you will be able to do it because you're in a position to make it happen. It's to do with promotion. There are galleries who have a greater significant presence than any of the artists they represent. We've harped on about that quite a bit, because it's maybe something that's not sufficiently taken into account. We're racing towards a situation where artists aren't all that important, 'important' galleries are.

Because the focus has shifted so much, the viewers can't trust their eyes, the artists themselves are self-interested, and critics keep changing their minds – it's called 're-assessing'. Gallerists have become the new priesthood. Unfortunately for us, on every level we are atheists.

T1+2 GALLERY

T1 + 2 Gallery was established in 2003 by it's Director Wolfe Lenkiewicz. Having met in Brick Lane we speak whilst walking around the local area.

How old is your gallery?
Five years. You see this building we are walking past now, that one was the first one I had. That nice old building was my gallery, but it was illegal.

Why's that?
I broke into it. As you can see this building was probably owned by a very wealthy man up in the North of England. But it was sitting here doing nothing for years. You can always tell them because they look very nice but they've got weeds growing out of them – do you see?

(Points to a batch of weeds growing out of the side of the building)

Yes...
And they've got these warnings saying that they're in security. It's got bars all along and steel doors.

Yes I see...
Well... how would you break in?

How would I break in?
Yes – to put on an art exhibition?

I've got no idea!
You see this security door. At the time they didn't have this security door

but a really strong outer wooden door. In broad daylight I went at it with an axe and broke the door open. So I was a little bit crazy. I went and turned the alarms off and I repaired the door and we put on a show called *100,000 Newspapers – A Public Active Installation* by an artist called Gustav Metzger. He was a very interesting artist of the sixties. He was an old man then and an even older one now.

How did you meet him?
I went out street drawing to pay for a gallery I started up with some friends. We counted up the coins and managed this way. It was hard work. Having laboured for months we had the gallery rent and in he walked. He sort of strayed in really like some cynic philosopher from ancient times or perhaps a bagman from modern times.

It was dangerous working on the street to make the rent. People would try and steal the hard-earned cash from my hat and I would have to fight them. We would punch each other and usually they would back off frightened of a sensitive artist. I would try to convince them that violence was ineffectual and try to talk about their appalling experiences in prison.

Anyhow, back to Metzger. Yes he wanted me to put a show of his on in a 'gallery' after I had written him a letter.

He happened to not want to deal with commercial galleries so it was perfect for him. He did not want to sell his work or show it in commercial galleries and for him the only way of getting his work seen morally or ethically was through an artist run space or to just not make art at all. So this seemed to be suitably dramatic and it was probably one of the largest spaces in the East End. It had huge amounts of space inside, we managed to get the electricity on and we had it for about six, maybe eight months before the landlord realised we were in there.

In fact I had a principle with all these galleries that I borrowed. We would always take the piano to the top floor. This kept us very fit and determined.

So I began by doing a huge show, involving or implying, that certain people were involved. Every single powerful person in the art world I somehow managed to get involved in the project because of that one person who was well known and had connections.

Meantime, I went along to the Atlantis gallery that was just over the road in the Truman Brewery and I got sponsorship from them, them not knowing I had a building down the road. They allowed me to use a huge sort of Turbine Hall-like scenario to have a conference. I invited people along which included the heads of different institutions, challenging all those different institutions, what they meant and what they could do for the art world at the time. I put a £2000 advert in Frieze, which I managed to get the money for from doing the paper drawings on the street. We had this show in the Atlantis gallery that went on for about two months. For the advert in Frieze I was cheeky, I phoned up people like Norman Rosenthal, Iwona Blaswick and I asked them if I could put their names on the advert in the sense that they sort of make an executive contribution toward the conference. Do you see? They turned up at the show and spouted crap like it's the best thing since the pyramids.

A lot of art-worldy people know nothing about art but they roll their r's like pimps and get very excited. We had open fires going and wartime telephones ringing and doors going nowhere. A lot of fun and very confusing for the poor souls until Mike Nelson came along and they found this entirely cosy.

Yes…
And they said "yeh sure put our names on". So I had a full-page advert that looked like some gallery had come out of the middle of nowhere and had every single person that was anyone in the art world endorsing it.

So the first thing is innovation, success really depends on it and a certain edginess I think. That's how it started. Then I broke into another building in Spitalfields.

Did you not get arrested for any of these?
No, but nearly. We had the whole place crawling with police. We found some tunnel under the ground and escaped into another building where

people were sleeping with a replica of Tutankhamen's mask above them.

And then I broke into another building in Spitalfields and I set up a gallery there for three years that was quite successful, though still not commercially. At this point I wasn't interested in making any money, nor did I know how.

So at this point nothing you had done had been for commercial gain?
No. You've got to realise that if you go back five years everything in the East End was artist-run. None of them knew how or at that point were trying to make money. They knew how to get Arts Council funding and some of them were better than others but they didn't know how to make money. In my case I felt a little exploited by Marxists sending me out on the street but I was forgiving of their selfish alcoholic and meta-mute British Petroleum funded magazines.

At this point Max Wigram came along and set up this show at the Royal Academy for all the different smaller galleries that hadn't been quite so known in the East End. That shot them into a different league. That was like a proto art fair before Zoo if you like. Frieze had only just begun because Frieze is only five years old. None of these main galleries would be able to afford to go into Frieze because they were all poor artist-run spaces. It was only when Zoo came along a few years later than Frieze that the artist-run spaces started realising that they could actually make some commercial headway, sell the artists and make a living out of it.

The landscape's changed. Any artist run spaces that are opening up now or any galleries are not like that. They're setting up immediately to be commercial. And they're not curatorial spaces either; they're not really intelligently curated. That's the difference. A few years ago there was a lot more initiative and it was more curatorial and now it's not.

Do you do both?
Well yes, but as it happens I hate curators and all there bull. You know Picasso and Lipsich put their own shows together. I was so aware of the 'Nu-Curators' but it just made me feel sorry for them to think of it. And I

do make a good job of the exhibitions that I put on and at the same time I make sure that they make money.

It's very difficult to predict how things are going to go anyway.

You mean with the market?
No with one's own career. It's hard as well. If an artist is doing performance or video it's much harder to sell.

Do artists need gallery representation?
Most artists that are worth their salt think hard about representation. Think heavily before you make that move and if you do ever sign a contract make sure it's a good offer.

So you don't represent artists?
How boring would it be to be restricted to a few artists whose work I have to repeat every year! This is one attitude I have considered but the problem with this is that you will eternally discover talent. Invest all your time and energy into it and other larger sharks will come along and scoop it up thanklessly.

Did you do well at the fair?
We made one hundred thousand in just a few days, but this is not common and one can't depend on it. Generally you just cut even. You watch though the scene will change again in a few years. In five years there will be no Frieze.

(Original recording inaudible now... but conversation continues on innovation, Damien Hirst's Freeze show – how he got the space for free – how he was supported by Michael-Craig-Martin who brought collectors and big names such as Saatchi and Serota along and that the exhibition was one of the first times artists' had produced a catalogue, which caught the attention of many.)

MATTHEW BOWN GALLERY

Matthew Bown Gallery is situated in London's West End. This conversation took place via email.

How old is the gallery and who set it up?
It is three years old and it was me who set it up. I am entirely privately funded.

Did you set up with the intention of becoming a commercial gallery? Did you have your list of collectors already? How did you get such a list?
Yes. Collectors you assemble as and how you can. Some are well known and so you phone their PA and ask for contact details. Others get in touch with you. Others come off of the street. Others you meet at art fairs.

Do certain galleries have certain collectors?
Some collectors have preferred galleries in the sense that they trust the advice of the owner.

Is there a certain rivalry between you and other galleries? Do you keep your collector list secure?
I keep everything secure. But it's not as big an issue as you think. Collectors buy what they want. If you have it, they'll buy it from you; if you don't, they will buy elsewhere.

How are collectors etc able to spot good art in today's growing contemporary market? Do they just rely on the reputation of a gallery?
Well, you hope they have their own eye. Obviously some people buy art at White Cube like they buy a suit in Armani, because of the brand. But they may not really know what they're doing.

What do collectors do with pieces once they have bought them?
Look at them and enjoy them I hope. Obviously big collectors have a storage/display problem.

Do you think the market affects what kind of art is produced?
Yes, up to a point; but it won't affect the best artists.

What is the difference between galleries in East London and galleries in West London?
I'm an East-End style gallery in the West-End. East-End is more grassroots.

Do you see the galleries in the East-End as competition? Are collectors buying from them now or is the most money still in the West?
If you mean a £50 million Picasso, that's still in West. Probably the same is true of Bill Viola or very top contemporary art. If you can afford to show those artists you can afford a West End space. No one is in the East End because they prefer it. Who prefers walking down Vyner Street to Bond Street? They're there because of lower overheads.

Do you only show works by the artists you represent?
No…

Do you ever take work by new artists?
Yes, if it's good.

How is demand created for a new artist?
Through consensus and an art world buzz.

Are installation or video works harder to sell?
Video no. Installation yes.

Are you keen to widen the audience for contemporary art?
No.

Who is your main audience?
The art-world.

If you take on an artist does that immediately elevate their status/ monetary value?
Maybe there is a knock-on effect from a show yes.

Do you think some galleries have greater reputation than the artists they represent?
The gallery's reputation is its artists.

How is value attributed to a work?
Value or price? Value is subjective I guess.

How is a price decided on?
What the market will accept. Not a science.

Do you think there is enough art criticism?
No.

ANONYMOUS

Here is a commercial gallery situated in London's West End. The Gallerist wished to remain anonymous. This conversation took place via email.

Do you get public funding or are you entirely privately funded?
We are entirely privately funded.

Did you set up with the intention of becoming a commercial gallery?
Yes…

Did you have your list of collectors already? And if so how did you get such a list?
Yes. Networking and years of building relationships.

Is there a certain rivalry between you and other galleries?
The contemporary art market is highly competitive.

How are collectors etc able to spot good art in today's wide contemporary market?
The definition of good art is subjective and depends on a wide range of criteria set by each collector. These maybe taste, motivations or art market trends.

Do collectors rely on the reputation of a gallery?
The reputation of the gallery may play an important part in their choice but it is not the only criteria, the quality of services provided by the gallery as well as the artwork presented are equally important.

Do you think the market affects what kind of art is produced?
No it does not affect what kind of art is produced but what kind of art is visible in the art market.

What is the difference between galleries in East London and galleries in West London? Do you see the galleries in the East End as competition?
The distinction between East and West London is not necessarily pertinent.

Do you only show works by the artists that you represent?
No...

Do you show any work by artists that you don't like?
No. In order to sell you have to appreciate the artwork or the artistic process that you are presenting.

Do you curate your shows?
Yes on most occasions.

Who is your main audience?
A wide range of people come into our gallery: students, artists, and professionals.

If you take on an artist does that immediately elevate their status/ monetary value?
We provide artists with a platform of quality that enable them to present their work to a wide range of public and collectors.

How is value attributed to a work?
Different variables are at play in the value attributed to artwork. These are: the value set by art market; value attributed by buyers and other criteria.

Do you attend art fairs?
Yes to increase visibility, strengthen networking with professionals, collectors and the public.

Do artists ever make new works especially for the fair?
Yes...

Would you be anywhere other than London?
Yes... *(New location omitted)*

DOMO BAAL

Director Domo Baal set up her gallery of the same name in 2000.

Can you tell me a bit about the gallery?
I set it up at the end of 2000 and the programme has been continuous since then. You're looking at show number fifty-two or fifty-three. I'd never previously worked in a gallery and was not really interested in the business that is the art world business. Although I have come to realise that the business side is quite important.

In 2004 I did an art fair on a whim. I had never done an art fair before as I went to one and didn't like it. I remember thinking "No, no, no, why would I do this?" I just didn't see the value of them. But I got invited to do an art show in Italy and I did it. Artissima is in Italy, and I love Italy. You learn a lot just by doing one but you fail miserably and it instantly clicks how the art world works. You have to develop the business side and you have to dovetail it with what you're doing curatorially. Ever since then it's changed certain key things in the business that is the gallery, while keeping content the clear agenda.

What were your intentions behind opening up a gallery?
I set it up in terms of creating a platform for art of a certain sensibility that I'm interested in and want to help develop as well as a certain dialogue that I want to develop. I don't want to follow whatever fashion is at the moment, but to strike out and assist in establishing certain practices. You could call it retrospectively more of a project space when I set it up – not that I was aware of those sorts of issues.

Where do you find your artists?
I approach people via their work and develop shows together with them. I

still work with some of those who I originally started working with. I only approach people through seeing their work, predominantly from art college, occasionally from elsewhere. I would never pinch artists from other galleries.

Do you represent artists?
I now represent artists that I can work with and that can work with me. My only golden rule, which is completely steadfast, is I have absolutely no niche. I'm not doing anything young and trendy. I have people with quite different profiles and I'm about to launch the career of a mature person who has never had a solo show. That's an example of how it can go very far from cool. Sian Pile is an example of someone who doesn't fit the predominant mould, but has an impressive and focused body of photographic work.

Some of the artists I have shown for quite some time now are beginning to get quite successful. That tends to be determined by curatorial success that then leads to straightforward business success. That's how I've been working up until now, as opposed to introducing people to collectors, which is possibly how other galleries maybe do it, I don't know.

Do you have a collector list?
I don't have a ready-made group of collectors who I am looking around for, as I really don't concentrate on that aspect at all. A lot of galleries seem to do that and that's something I've come to learn. And that's fine I mean it's a very successful business model. But you might end up being a scout for what your collectors like because what your collectors like is very important, which could be dangerous. I am slowly now, developing relationships with collectors who are seeking to build serious focused collections. That is extremely rewarding in every way.

Do you think that collectors can influence what art is made or put out there?
Yes definitely, of course, they are the fuel in the machine. The youngest artist in the gallery was selected for a show at the Venice Biennale and I've now sold almost every single work she's ever made and they've mostly gone to major collections.

There's nothing like that for teaching you how collectors work. Some introduce their favourites, who don't have galleries. So there is a huge amount of pressure from collectors who have spent heavily with the gallery to do a certain thing. That is maybe understandable but I would completely refuse. That obscures my way of thinking which for me is critical because if I don't relate to it, I then lose my own response, which is always my starting point. I have to relate to it to start the process of thinking about wanting to have it in my gallery. If I don't relate to it it's not going in. I think it's a very, very dark world but very rich in terms of it's variety and I have absolutely no intention to add to the volume. I want to develop a particular voice.

I think that's really quite admirable. Do you think many others have the guts to do that anymore?
Well I'm older than a lot of the others as I'm over fifty. I wanted to run a gallery for years and couldn't work out how to do it other than that the business side is very important. Especially as a show like this costs a lot of money and is not exactly an easy seller, as aren't other shows I do. So when you're thinking how do I finance it then sales are an obvious route. If you start thinking of that it's no more or less complicated than running any other business that needs investment. But when you're older you get either more selfish or less worried about what other people think. But certainly success with some artists has given a lot of confidence not just to me but also to the artists themselves as well as to other artists who show with the gallery.

So you're saying one of the reasons you became commercial is to help fund the shows you put on?
I don't do anything now than I didn't before other than I became aware that you have to sell in order to fund what you do. I don't have a backer, I have been approached by them and as much as it's nice to have someone to pay the bills I don't want to be coerced into showing or taking the latest trendy thing and then dropping them, which is what I see a lot of galler-

ies do a lot of. It's just not what I'm interested in. Artists I work with who work with other galleries tell me I give more freedom than other galleries do within an artist's practice to do what they want to achieve the show that they want.

Can an artist's practice be dictated by the market?
Yes, and that's understandable, but also dangerous. That's clearly a road to nowhere. I didn't change what I do but the things I did start to sell were to people who had stuck with my gallery and looked at things from the very beginning. It sometimes takes a long time to develop a buying relationship and that appears to be because buyers are looking at an artist and waiting for the artist to develop. So I have frequently sold things that I had shown them three years previously. And sometimes you think how silly because it's very often that a person has bought something at two or three times the price two or three years later. It's happened about four times now that someone's asked me the price and I say that the artist has recently graduated. Then there's been notable success within a career and then the prices go up. Then someone who's seen it in 2001, last year bought work that was £10,000 when I showed it originally for £1300, without even complaining. It might well be people who are building up a serious collection or sometimes buying with other people's money, and therefore exercising caution, who do this.

So they wait for a reputation to grow?
Yes, for them to be sure and to give them the extra confidence. We know that a lot of artists who leave art school are not practicing as artists five years later simply because it is a very difficult thing to do. And collectors are very aware of that. They've often been looking for far longer and they are aware of that statistic and that they may be watching someone who stops making art or doesn't develop. I mean you might buy it because you like it and I wish everyone did that but it's not always the case and you can't count on it. So you have to find something that's going somewhere. So there's a lot of looking and a lot of questions at an early stage even when it doesn't lead to buying.

How would the value of a work increase?
Pricing is complicated or rather you've got to pitch it right. You can't just put on what you want; you've got to be very aware of what other people do. Everyone knows what he or she can buy in contemporary art for £1000. People who are buying art know what they can buy for £1000, £2000, £10,000, £50,000. They know who sells at what price in terms of what artist and they have comparables. A lot of artists seem to think this cost me a year to do therefore it costs a fortune. That consideration unfortunately, has no place in the equation of the way things are priced. So when an artist does begin to sell and does begin to sell out – and I've got two artists who've sold almost everything they've done – that does push prices up, especially when they start selling to public collections and international, high profile collections.

(She points)

Behind there is an A3 copy of a woodcut that I showed. She's now left the gallery and we didn't sell a single thing and didn't get reviews. But people said "wow" and her woodcuts then sold to MoMA New York two years later, and to the Albertina in Vienna. So then slowly people started creeping forward. I did another show and the work began to sell. The same work I showed in her first show went up in price, and in the main sold out.

How did someone from the MOMA become aware of something shown here?
It had a write up in the Guardian Guide. The MOMA acquisition took approximately twelve to fifteen months of various committee meetings and questions that needed answering. She was also invited to do a solo show at the Ikon Gallery in Birmingham. So everything good that happens to an artist's work after they graduate can potentially add into the value of the work.

Is the rise in value and acclaim subjective?
It all has to be subjective but you have to get a consensus of subjectivities.

One person saying it's great isn't enough unless it's someone amazing who really has power but even then it takes more. Ideally work is accepted and applauded in several different ways, curatorially, critically and sales-wise, with a variety of exhibition inclusions. That's beginning to happen with this piece *(then showing at the gallery)* you can just feel it. *Time Out* gave this show the 'pick of the week' review. I've been asked to show it in Chicago in April and about five youth magazines that I've never even heard of and online organisations have turned up. And I've had a gallery full of twenty-two year old guys asking to film it to put it online. It's when you get that ground swell of all different kinds of people clearly interested and staying that you know it's likely to do very well.

You mentioned that you didn't come with a list of collectors. Do most galleries start with one in order to function as a business?
I think a lot do. I do know that a lot of people who set up galleries have worked in other galleries before. One of the points of working for a gallery would seem not just learning the principles of how a gallery is run but also making those relationships. You are not going to walk off with any artists, although some might, but it's about those other relationships that are not just collectors but the press, curatorial and all those kind of things. Critics and writers are also important and I've just built my list up organically.

I know you show really quite different works but do you think it's possible to almost spot a pattern in other places and in what they're showing?
Yes, and I steer away from that. But yes I think you can and that's why I quite like being geographically somewhere different. Certain galleries have their preferences and certain artists they've worked with for ages but I do find that one of the disadvantages of being in an area with very few galleries is that few visitors pop in on the off chance. On the other hand, an advantage might be that you don't get submerged in the East End look. I think we've all done it, every now and then I go on a Sunday and they sort of become a blur. You can divide them into two you know, the scruffier spaces and the more hard core, but basically it becomes a blur. I'm wary of

that and being in a separate geography I think is very useful, although a challenge. What's the point of doing what everyone else does?

So you mean if you were situated amongst many others you'd be tempted to look at or follow what everyone else is doing?
Perhaps yes. But it's again collector led. Collectors just go to all of the galleries and there is nothing like starting to sell that could stimulate a certain pressure. You might feel you need to keep the collectors happy. I feel that pressure and I just don't like it. For example, certain collectors are starting to buy across artists that I show and that is lovely. Yet when they turn up and they see something they hate and then start to question my judgment that's quite worrying and at the same time it tests you. You have to justify what you show to yourself as well as to others. I don't have a single artist who doesn't get invited to exhibit elsewhere. I work very hard at placing them in other shows in other galleries. I've got at least eight or nine consignment notes from my gallery for totally different kind of shows at other galleries, a museum in Germany, an artist run space in Bratislava, something in LA, at any one time.

You talk about the East-End clusters and the West-End clusters. What would you say the main difference is between spaces in the East and in the West?
Well money is the obvious one. The more money there is invested whether in the space or the production level the less risk anyone can take. At the same time the fairly dull moneyed West End spaces might have had a problem where they've had to create a bit of buzz and money is not that buzzy; money is always very conservative. If it's buying wacky contemporary art it's buying wacky contemporary art because a brand has been achieved out of an artist or a gallery, which allows certain collectors to feel safer that there money has been well spent. There is no difference other than that the East End are kind of selling experimentation or risk as a concept. But there's not a single one of them that wouldn't invest more money if they had it, so there's no real difference really.

The places I have spoken to with the huge money involved...
Are very cagey. [Anon] has invented a whole vocabulary that few use. I
don't know if you've noticed but in my experience some never actually use
the words "buy" and "sell" they talk about "placing; that can be as accurate
as it is pompous. It might be about building up a mystique around things
that are actually very obvious. When you're working at a level where you've
got salaries and rent is a fortune you have to make quite a lot of money. At
different levels you might have to make £50,000 or £100,000 a week and
that has to come from somewhere and that only comes from sales. And so
the constraints at that level, the running of an art gallery has nothing to do
with art; it's straightforward business concerns. That equation has to balance
otherwise they go under.

There must be a lot less freedom for the artist when working like that?
Yes definitely. When you're not making money or when you're starting there
is nothing, whether you're an artist or a gallery. In my experience starting
out as a gallery is not very different from starting as an artist where you
basically do what you want to do and hope it works. On a simple level you
concentrate on what your project is but until that voice is heard be it by
collectors, critics, whoever, you have freedom to develop it. Freedom is scary
but you can develop it. It's once that voice is heard in the big galleries, once
collectors buy, that it becomes a powerful tool in the business. Most big galleries who are successful will tell you that there are only six or eight people
in the world who really buy art big time at any one time and they have to
do work with those people because otherwise they have no business. When
they're putting together a show that might cost tens of thousands just for the
production cost of the show, that cash has to come from somewhere.

Do you think the audience for art should be as wide as possible?
Definitely; with absolutely no restrictions. That is the one thing galleries
can do. And in these days where there are lots of different ways of acquiring
art, where everything's very accessible, where you've got the Internet, open
studios, art schools, and artist-run spaces, the one thing all galleries can do is

create a sort of thinking space. They can create platform where an artist can develop a body of work to be shown in a specific way at a specific time in a specific place, which is then opened up to the widest audience possible.

But do you think this wide audience comes in?
Well of course it's a tough challenge and you can't make them because people go around with Time Out and we're competing with every football match, every restaurant and everything you can do on a Saturday or whenever. That's fine but in the end those who are interested find you. I get groups of young people from colleges. There is a wide and varied audience. There is nothing, even if you're very hard nosed and only aiming at your collector, there is nothing more off putting than someone who is seriously thinking of buying coming to see a show where there is nobody in it.

I guess that's the same with any of the arts isn't it?
Yep. The test of a good show is when people come back. That's my litmus test, when they come back just to look a week or two later. That happens here routinely with particular artists, not necessarily those who've followed the artists' work previously, but equally from people who've seen it for the first time.

Do you think there is enough art criticism around now?
No. Not real criticism. It's a very difficult thing to do well. There can only be a few really good artists and writing about art well and adding something without killing it off, or over explaining it is a very difficult thing to do. It's not just about what your opinion is it's how you justify it and how it stacks up against what else is out there. It's difficult to do and very few people do it very well. There's a successful and strong market out there and the magazines are essentially cliquey self-interest groups who are supporting their own. So they will talk out what they want to talk out, it's not really criticism. We've all got people who we like, who we read, who manage to say something that literally comes from thinking as opposed to quite a lot of people who just explain work in writing and then you think "yeh but what

do you think?" There might be veiled subtexts in that maybe they wouldn't write about it if they didn't like it. But that has to be the least interesting thing about any work of art, what it is doing. The interesting thing is always why and how.

I find it really odd actually. It used to be a convention that if something was a best seller, or extremely popular, not in art particularly, but in music or books, it was rarely something good, popularity itself was kind of disparaging. There was a sort of "oh it's a best seller it can't be really good". But in art if you get someone who is doing well commercially and financially, it's now a given that it's good. It gets beyond sort of criticism and beyond certain people questioning if it's good or not. And I find that a very curious paradox. If something does well, that is to be applauded because it's a difficult thing to do – no matter what they do or whether their work is good or not or contributes to a dialogue that is contemporary art at the moment – but those are separate issues. And that's what art criticism should do and it is very rare.

ONE IN THE OTHER

One in the Other was set up by Chris Noraika.
It is a commercial gallery located on Vyner Street.

Can you tell me a bit about how the gallery was set up?
The gallery has been through a process of change. It didn't start out as a
gallery but has been running as a gallery for about four years. It started off
as a project space. I was studying fine art, making my own work and along
with some other people who I was at college with we put on a show. I then
became interested in taking it further so I started to put on other shows,
not of my own work but of other peoples. That was in 1996.

   The first show that we did was in a disused shop in Exmouth market. I was in the first show along with two other people and then we did
one more show in Exmouth market. The third show, which was at Tenter
Ground, I didn't actually participate in myself. I was more interested in
other peoples work. So it started off as just one show and we didn't have a
programme of any description we just went from one show to the next in a
roll-on sequence of collaborations.

So it wasn't commercial when it first set up?
No not at all. Not until we left there and went to a space near Wharf road.
At that time it went through a sort of transition and we became aware of
the commercial implications of running a space. By that I mean to run a
space it costs money, you can only do it for so long unless it's self-gener-
ating. So there were three cycles to the gallery: the origins, then Tenter
Ground and then the space here on Vyner Street.

Are you now entirely self-funded?
Yes there's no public funding or anything, it's just a business.

What is your opinion on the Vyner Street phenomenon and what are the negative or positive aspects of having so many galleries together?
I think it's pretty good. I mean in London terms it feels like there's a lot in one area because traditionally everything has been spread out. But if you compare it to other places in other countries, especially New York, it's no big deal. You have ten galleries in one street and there are 300 galleries in one district in Chelsea. So just a few in and around Bethnal Green is in that context, not a big deal.

But people do respond to it and they respond to it well. Instead of trekking all over London they can go to one gallery, then another and if you can help by grouping a few together then people will appreciate that. I think it makes sense because the East End is traditionally an area where artist-run spaces colonise. Also, the East End is a very large area so you've always got loads going on that feeds it. Vyner Street becomes symbolic of that.

Do you visit many of the galleries in this street?
Yes…

Do you think that this has an effect on the kind of art that you show? Are you influenced by what you see going on around you?
I think that all galleries have their own programme; they've all got their own agenda. I think they're looking at youngish emerging UK and International artists but each one has their own particular take on that. I've not been aware of a doubling up of people's programmes. Everyone has their own particular variation and you see the richness and diversity of that. There are similarities in that they're looking to work with young emerging artists but that's all.

I have spoken to some people who say they see a lot of things that seem quite similar?
Anthony Wilkinson is on a different scale to a lot of the others in Vyner Street so you know there's no comparison there at all. Modern Art is still on Vyner Street and they have little in common with a lot of the other galleries;

they've grown out of the East End quite a lot. If you take Kate MacGarry, what she does is take on artist's work which is really specific and there is no similarity between there, Fred upstairs or David Risely. Fred again has a very particular identity to his gallery programme.

I think for someone to say that means that they are almost coming to the conclusion that all artists and all galleries on a much wider scale all share a similarity. And I think that if someone is coming to that conclusion, if they deduce or conclude that a lot of contemporary art is similar, then that is fine. But I think Vyner Street is just an example of that.

Personally I don't share that view, I don't think there's a sort of Vyner Street aesthetic or sensibility that if you have a gallery in Vyner Street you will make art or show art in a particular way. If someone comes along and says "oh this all looks the same to me" then they have to extend the logic of that and say that all galleries are showing work that is quite similar. On the one hand you could say that, if you simplify what people are doing, you can find some sort of common denominator. But if you look at the different nuances then actually there is no similarity at all.

Do you think there is any rivalry between galleries or the galleries in Vyner Street?
Not specifically Vyner Street but there is rivalry amongst galleries in general. You could say we're bunched together so these are your competitors. People might argue that but it doesn't manifest itself in a kind of rivalry, I would say in Vyner Street it's the opposite. I'm not saying we meet for group hugs and meetings all the time, but there is a sort of shared unspoken pursuit.

Do you think there is still a division between the East End and the West End spaces?
I think it's very different. It's not to say they don't overlap in areas. There are some galleries in the East End who market themselves as a more refined blue-chip operation and they wouldn't be out of place in some West End locations. You could think of the East End as being more cutting edge in that they are prepared to work more with younger artists who are at a rawer

stage in their career whereas West End galleries are less inclined to do that and they'll concentrate on more established artists. However, now there are some East End galleries who work with more established artists and some West End who work with younger artists. So it is blurring.

Do you think the art market effects what kind of art is produced or shown?
I think it can be very influential. It's such a conspicuous presence and I think it plays a bigger role in what happens now than it ever did in the past. I think it is inevitable that that will filter into what sort of work gets made or what sort of work gets exposure. It's hard to get inside the minds of artists though and it's hard to know exactly how that influence manifests itself.

Is endorsement based on subjective taste and do you think all the promotion and endorsement is done for the right reasons?
I don't think galleries sell work just because it sells. Adopting a kind of commercialism at all costs stands out a mile. Work that doesn't have integrity; that isn't rigorous; that hasn't been honed over a period of time or been part of the right decision-making stands out a mile. What I do think people do is that they look for work that meets all of those criteria and also has a place within the market. Galleries are businesses so they will look to promote artists whose work they feel has a place within the art market.

Do you think that it's possible to spot trends in the market?
Every now and again people say "oh I'm going to buy a lot of photography" or "I'm going to buy a lot of painting". There are clear trends and whether you can kind of predict them or create them I don't know. East German paintings were very popular recently. Polish art and Chinese art are becoming popular. But these things have integrated into our culture and the emergence of these may not necessarily be market craze. It maybe that world culture is evolving so things come to prominence. Chinese art is due to the prominence that China is coming to on the global stage as well as an economic and cultural force.

When you go to other art galleries or art fairs do you still get excited about the work you see?
I think there is really good work out there. I mean there's clearly works that I prefer over others and there's work I respect but don't necessarily like. I have work that I don't think is good at all for very particular reasons but I'm aware that that's my personal discourse on it and other people might not share that. So no I don't think that it's all 'anything goes'. I don't think the standards have slipped.

Do you think there's enough art criticism?
It's a difficult time for it, I'm not sure it knows what it's doing or where it's going or what it's role is. Art criticism has been usurped by the art market. I think in the past criticism had a crucial role to play in informing people what was good and bad because they needed to know about work. But now people don't look to art criticism anymore, people look to the art market. Instead they think "well who's selling and who isn't?" You could have a sell out show, work selling for millions of pounds and it will be totally panned by the critics and writers; Damien Hirst is a perfect example.

Criticism is clearly not having an influence on people; people are still happy to buy. On the one hand you've got commercial success but you've not got critical success. That's been a long-standing phenomenon. Art criticism just feels like journalism, I don't think it's particularly great. It won't be looked back on as a particularly great time for art criticism; I think it's a bit lost to be honest. It's by-the-yard-stuff and it gets just churned out and put out there.

There's no real voice and maybe that's just because it's impossible to do. There's a real multiplicity of the times, there is no one prevailing viewpoint. It's not like Modernism, Post Modernism or Expressionism; it's just anything you know. So it's hard to give a complete view on it and have a clear voice.

So there are works that may not have won over any critical acclaim but are selling for thousands or millions of pounds. Why is that?
Take Hirst. Hirst is a brand; it's impervious to art criticism. It's an asset, a

commodifiable asset. It's status is so strong it can withstand what art criticism says about it and the only thing that will affect it will be market forces. So if everyone woke up one day and thought "you know what I don't think Hirst is worth that much I'm going to sell it". If everyone started trying to sell his work then the value of it would come down. That's the only kind of thing that would change and that works no different from the housing market or any other type of market asset.

But why is it so strong in the first place, is it power?
No it's market forces that do that. It's an accumulative thing. In the beginning Hirst was a really good artist and made good work so it wasn't just built on a myth. But money takes over and people get drawn into the machinations of that and into a gallery system that represents and has a list of wealthy clients, and as a result such artists' work become immensely successful commercial products.

Who do you think the audience for art should be?
It can be anyone and everyone will take away something different. People don't have to agree on it, every experience is legitimate.

Why attend art fairs?
It's a very efficient way of accessing collectors large and small and a way of communicating what the gallery does to a broader, more mixed audience.

When collectors seek out art do they look to a reputed gallery first and trust them do you think or do they look for artists?
Collectors like to build up a certain trust with galleries, as they like to feel confident in what they are doing and in the artists that they are showing. That comes over time so as a result of that they may tend towards galleries they know, that they're familiar with, but not to the exclusion of all others. A lot of the time they're out there looking for something different that they can't find from other galleries. We work with clients on a regular basis and that's good because you build up a dialogue and you can go to them and say

"look I think you'll really like this stuff". That's why Zoo art fair exists. You can go to Frieze for your established names but people come to Zoo as well to find artists they don't know about or a gallery they haven't heard of yet.

How do you decide what to take to an art fair?
You just take what you believe is your strongest work.

KINETICA

Kinetica, founded by Dianne Harris, Tony Langford and Charlotte Dillon is both a museum and a gallery dedicated to showing multi-disciplinary art. Here I am in conversation with Operations Manager Peter McCormack.

Can you tell me a bit about Kinetica?
Dianne Harris, Tony Langford and Charlotte Dillon established Kinetica as an organization in the summer of 2006. It first opened to the public on October 6th 2006.

Can you explain a bit about how Kinetica functions as both an art gallery and museum?
As a museum, Kinetica presents innovative and pioneering work in a historical context, creating a forum that encourages discussion and direct engagement with both artists and audiences. As a gallery, Kinetica directly supports the development of new art and artists through the sale and promotion of work in the exhibitions.

Can you tell me a bit about your relationship with the Arts Council? Were you entirely funded by them at one point? You mentioned in an earlier conversation we had that they were pushing you to become commercial. Can you say why and how this affects Kinetica?
The Arts Council was a major sponsor of Kinetica and continues to help fund various programmes. But it has never been our only source of funding. While our commercial activities are not eligible for direct funding assistance from the Arts Council, they are encouraged as they provide the means for better self-sustainability and less reliance on public funds.

Is expanding your commercial aspect positive or negative?
The commercial aspect of the organisation involves different areas such as the newly launched shop and Kinetica's increased fair activity. So the association is completely positive as it increases the level of exposure but does not determine or interfere with the curatorial approach or range of programs offered through the museum.

While these aspects will not affect the work publicly shown in exhibitions or acquired for Kinetica's permanent collection, commercial factors will naturally influence the kind of work sold through the shop and fairs where market trends will play an unavoidable role.

Do you represent artists?
Kinetica does represent artists but not in an exclusive manner. We will negotiate sales and new commissions on behalf of artists, dealers and other galleries but we are not limited to promoting only those with whom we are associated. There is no bias or commercial agenda behind the artists Kinetica selects for its exhibitions.

Is there any rivalry between you and other galleries?
There is always some rivalry for funding as sources are quite limited but this does not really involve any specific institution or organization.

Do you think the art market affects what kind of art is produced?
Ultimately the answer is yes no matter how much we may want it to be a non-factor. But I think there are a number of ways to positively influence the market. By providing an opportunity for the widest possible audience to discover and engage with such work, documenting the processes involved and presenting it in a manner that clearly demonstrates the historical context, influence and importance, the market becomes less fickle, like a well informed patron rather than a respondent to fashion.

What is the difference between galleries/spaces in East London and galleries in West London?
Location! Just kidding. I think the primary difference is that the East End has been associated with a more provocative, less commercial involvement with the arts. That may have involved the artist and the work being produced, the aims of the gallery, the artist communities that developed because of a relatively inexpensive workspace in the East, or even the social programs aimed at giving a voice to disenfranchised communities.

Are you keen to widen the audience for contemporary art?
I think every institution within the arts would like to widen its audience but Kinetica is particularly interested in the cross-fertilization of ideas that result from interdisciplinary approaches and international dialogue.

Who do you think arts audience should be?
Everyone should have access and be encouraged to engage with the arts in whatever capacity they choose.

CYNTHIA CORBETT GALLERY

The Cynthia Corbett Gallery was established by former Christie's Education Art History graduate Cynthia Corbett and is operated from her Victorian home, a former convent, with high ceilings and massive rooms.

Can you tell me a bit about The Cynthia Corbett Gallery? How old is it, what was its original conception etc...
Well I didn't start off in the art world. I was from a largely Italian-American, very cultured background and although I never did art myself I have always loved art and music.

I began my career working in New York as an International Economist. I had a degree in International Relations and Political Science and was working in emerging markets helping developing countries work on their problems. I was transferred to London by the bank that I was working for to work with African countries. Whilst here I met my husband and decided to stay. We had a daughter who I was always dragging around to museums and churches in any country or city that we went to.

Between seven and nine my daughter started to have problems at school and I thought that it was because of all my work and travelling. So I quit my job and went back to college to study art history. I had already studied history and I loved politics and art so I just thought that this would be great for me to do. And that was my transformation.

I looked at all of the courses and thought that Christies had a brilliant educational program. I did two years with them and got a diploma. We had to sell our old house to fund all of my education and so we moved into this apartment where you are sitting. When we moved in here it was a converted convent and basically a dump. We did a lot of work and my fellow classmates from Christie's came and said "well why don't you have a gallery here?" They had known that I wanted a gallery.

And you did...
Well it made sense because all of the walls had picture rails and it is a lateral house as opposed to an up and down house. There are a lot of walls and a lot of big rooms with high ceilings. I thought "ok I'll try it".

That was in 2000 and I didn't know what I was doing. When people ask me when I established the gallery I say 2000, but officially it was more 2003. It was 2003 because it took me over three years, and I'm still learning, still trying to understand what a gallery is. I had never worked in a gallery and I had no idea about the business of art. I just knew I loved art.

I was lucky because studying at Christies meant that I had some exposure to the art market, it's movement and some practicalities. But you don't know anything about a gallery and the gallery business until you've run one.

Because I have a business background and I'm very presentable Christies people were asking why didn't I apply to Christies or Sotheby's or work for a big gallery. I realised that I would have had to start so low, and I had childcare considerations, so I thought no – I want to try and do this myself. And that's why I started the gallery myself.

So obviously we're in your house, which looks great with the art hanging everywhere. What affect do you think the home environment has on the work you show and the people who come and see it?
Oh I think it is very positive. No one has been negative. It helps the people who are less familiar with art galleries, who are not big collectors or those who are just starting out. They love coming to a home environment because it's not intimidating and they can picture things in their own home or office. People also love seeing the way we can put very contemporary pieces with very old furniture, antiques or painted furniture. It helps people take risks in their own collecting or in their own buying. So it's been very positive.

We mostly invite people or it is by appointment. There have been a few people who just ring the doorbell and say that they're here to see something and you just go "oh my God, ok" – but that's not often, just because it's a home gallery.

So are your main audience collectors and buyers as opposed to the general public?
Yes for sure. One-hundred-percent. This is not a public gallery. It couldn't be because it is a private home in an area where we live. I can't open to the general public and I wouldn't be allowed to.

Do you not think it's important that people other than just buyers and collectors get to see the work?
Well they can call if they want to. I've had people call up and that's fine. They're not forbidden I just mean that we can't put a sign up. But of course people come, I've had a couple of people come this summer for instance. Not everyone that comes here is going to collect and buy. I had Tate patrons here, a whole group of them. They just came and had lunch and looked around. They were curious to see how a home gallery worked and so they put me on their visiting list.

That's a nice crowd to have over for lunch!
Yes, really cool.

Geographically you are based in Wimbledon and so quite a way from the centre of London. Do you think that this has an affect on you at all?
It has some affect in perception I think more than it does in practicality. There is a perception that I'm in Wimbledon so I must be a Wimbledon gallery – whatever that means. But how did you get here?

From Waterloo
Yes, Waterloo. And you see it's twelve minutes. So actually it is not very far at all and it's not very hard to get here. It's closer than say Brooklyn to Manhattan, which takes twenty minutes. The distance doesn't prevent anyone going to Wimbledon College of Art, which is very cool, very cutting edge and one of the best colleges in London.

So no I'm not in the East End and I'm not in central London. But neither am I in the small group of galleries that are just in Wimbledon Village; I don't fit in with them at all. At all. I mean they are fine and they are nice people and they show nice art but I have a programme that is really quite contemporary, very ambitious and very international. And they don't. So I'm much more like a central London Gallery. Much more.

Sometimes one of my collectors who for example met me in Italy or Spain says "oh sorry I'm only here two days I can't come to Wimbledon". But that's ok because usually when they are here it's for a big art fair and usually I'm in central London showing anyway.

I'm always all over the place exhibiting. Having a home gallery has meant that I don't have to have big overheads like a central London gallery which would kill me. It gives me the ability to do other things internationally that I would not be able to do if I had to find the rent for a central gallery. I don't think I'd still be going if I were renting somewhere, as the rent is too huge. The West is something like one hundred and twenty thousand pound a year. So what do you think you have to sell in a year to make that?!

Well that accounts for the huge prices…
You have to sell about five-hundred-thousand pounds worth of art a year just to cover your costs and make anything. That's just what you have to sell! So you know if you are selling Banksy, Damien Hirst or Lucian Freud then you don't have to worry about it. But if you're selling young emerging artists then how are you going to do that? How are you going to do that unless you have a huge backer? And I don't have backing. I've never received backing from anyone.

Has anyone offered to back you?
No. Though I have been looking for a backer, partner or patron desperately since about 2003.

Who would that be? A collector…?
It would be good to have a collector that liked my taste and my concept.

They could be a lover of the arts or a former banker. It could be a former lawyer or somebody who had made a lot of money as a hedge fund manager and who is interested in supporting a gallery. I wasn't on the wealthy side of banking you see, I wasn't a banker, I was just an economist, a staff person. I made a normal salary and not all of this bonus money that you hear about people getting. I had a really great friend in Boston who was willing to back me but I would have had to stay there and that wasn't really practical.

Do you worry that if you were to have a backer that would influence the work you show?
No…

Do you think that there are differences between the types of spaces that operate in the East End and West End of London?
Yes. I like what the East End is and I'm going to be doing a show there. I did one show there before, in Redchurch Street. It was of Yvonne de Rosa.

Did you rent the space then?
Yes and I'm doing it again in the Maverik Showroom. We love the East End and we had a wonderful experience there. People loved what we were doing so we decided to go back this October. We have been chosen out of all the eighty galleries that are participating in the East End festival for Photo-month to launch it at Maverik Showrooms. Photomonth is in conjunction with *Timeout* and the Whitechapel Gallery.

So that will be my second project in the East-End and then next year I will do hopefully two or three more because I love it and I think it's very vibrant. But it's not right for all of my artists. It's not right for her *(points to work of Anne Françoise Couloumy)*. Anne Françoise Couloumy needs to be in the West End. I just had a big show for her on Cork Street in June and that was really well received.

Who is she?
She's a very well known French Artist and collected by amazingly success-

ful and well-known celebrities in France. She's not that well known here yet because no one shows her work here in London. When I saw her work I said I loved it and wanted to show her here in London. She didn't really care. She's just won the French equivalent of a CBE and had no need to show in London. But I worked on her since 2001 and we established a very good relationship and she agreed. So I showed her a few times at different art fairs and I had a show for her here and it went really well. That was in 2004.

Then in 2006 I rented a tiny little gallery space in the village of Wimbledon for the two weeks during the tennis so that I got all the international traffic. I didn't mind getting Wimbledon people if you see what I mean but I wanted the international traffic and I got it. This year I asked if she were ready to do a major show in London and she was and she did all this new work just for London. To follow on from that we are taking just her to Art London in Chelsea. Again this work will appeal to a lot of international people who might live in Chelsea and Kensington – so she's going to become better known.

So for me the answer is yes there is a difference. I think there is dynamism and youngness in the East that I just love. One of the things I'm going to try and do there next year is a video show. Just video. I adore video. I could never chance something like that in Cork Street because the price of the hiring is so high that the pressure on me to sell would be too great. The risk would be too great and my gallery could go under. Whereas if I didn't sell in the East-End yes I would lose money but I wouldn't lose so much that I couldn't then operate or couldn't do my next show.

I think it's really interesting that you have a base here and yet you can go to all these different places and have what is essentially your gallery there as well. It's sort of an itinerant…
I'm a roving gallery. And I think that if people like you bother to actually have a proper conversation with me about it they will see that in a way I am probably spending a lot.

A lot of people say "oh you don't have any overheads you just have your gallery in your own home". Well yes if I just sat here and did this but even then I would still spend money because I would be promoting my artists. I'm not just sitting here. The reason I'm still using my home is because it gives me the opportunity to go to the East-End when it's an appropriate exhibition, to go to the West-End when it's and appropriate exhibition and likewise, go overseas.

My artists are so lucky because some of them, Tom Leighton for example, I take overseas. I showed him in Chicago and New York before he had even graduated from art-college just because I liked his work and I thought I should take it. I was taking other artists that had sold well before and were better known yet we sold him well too because his work was so great. But a lot of galleries won't make that commitment to go overseas because it is so expensive and it is so risky.

I'm making as much of a commitment to my artists as I would if I had a gallery that I was sitting in everyday on a main street somewhere. It's just I do things differently. I have to be international. I couldn't spend all my money just having a gallery in London – even though London's great. I have to be somewhere else as well because I'm such an international. I got my degree in International Relations and I have always travelled around the world constantly. And as soon as I was doing my art history diploma and we went on trips I knew that I had to somehow get overseas for my artists.

If it wasn't for practical reasons would your gallery be based anywhere else?
I would have my gallery in New York in a minute. I'm from Boston not New York but really my whole life as a young girl was in New York. That's where I lived, that's where I developed my first career, that's where my friends are. So I love New York and New York is very prominent. What I would ideally like to do is have a gallery there and in London. I would also like to have a close relationship with a gallery or space in Paris because Paris was the first place I went to look at art. Also Paris for me is most important historically for the Modern period of art, say from 1850/60. So I love Paris and I love the way Parisian people and collectors generally love and appreciate art. I love that. I'm a Francophile. So if I could I would

have a gallery in London, I'd have something in New York and something in Paris. And maybe one day I will.

Do you represent artists?
Yes that's what I do. I say that I do art consulting and I would if someone approached me – a bank, a company or a collector. But my main focus is representing artists. I find artists that I want to work with. If they come to me and I like them I will work with them. I only represent artists and try to have a relationship with artists whose work I really connect with. I know when I see a work that I love because I'm drawn to it or it moves me. That can be for a variety of reasons; it may be aesthetically or because of the darkness, the political, or the cleverness. It must be something that I think I want to show.

Where do you find your artists?
Everywhere. I go to all of the degree shows I have time for and I'm also out all of the time, looking and looking. I go to other galleries, public shows, international shows or people's friends. But most of the people I represent came from graduate shows that I saw.

I will approach them and try to work with them but it doesn't always work. I might love the art but either the artist doesn't want to work with me or the chemistry isn't right. Just like a relationship – you might look at someone and go "wow I love that persons looks" but then you don't get on. But my first thing will be the work and then I hope that the relationship with the artist will work and that they will trust me and I will trust them. I hope they respect me realise I am nurturing them. I think I am quite a maternal figure in my character and I like being able to see people doing well and help them and market them.

Are all the works that you show works that you like?
Only. Only. Only. People say to me "what kind of work do you show? Only Conceptual or..." No. I show what I like. I don't have to justify myself to anybody. I love her painting *(points to the work of Anne Françoise*

Couloumy), she reminds me of Vermeer and Hopper. And I don't really care if someone says to me how could you show that with that. I have a projector up here *(points)* set up for outside video art, next to this classical painting.

If someone is the greatest artist in the world and they tell me "oh I'm so great and I've sold all this stuff'" or if someone says "my friend, they've just come out of Camberwell" or wherever, "she's amazing"; if I don't like it I am not showing it. Because there is nothing worse than a gallery who is showing work and exhibiting artists that they don't believe in. I couldn't sell it. I just couldn't talk about it.

Do you think that happens then, that galleries do that?
Yes. I know who they are. You can tell when you go on a stand who they are. I don't actually begrudge them and I'm not going to be overly critical of someone – I just can't do that. I could never do it. One time someone came to me and they said they knew this amazing artist. I said ok and it was awful, absolutely awful. I was thinking "you go sell it, I can't". The whole experience was so awful because I knew I just didn't believe in the artist. And it didn't mean that the artist was bad, the artist was fine.

Well if you're not passionate about it you can't really talk passionately about it can you...?
No. It even happens with some of the artists who I love and I think are my babies. If they come up with some works that I don't like, I actually have to say "I can't sell that". I mean we can show it and funnily enough one of my assistants who was working with me said "oh I love that" and I said "Ok fine. Go for it, but keep me away because I will cost the gallery a sale". Because people know. So it is very personal.

Do you ever feel any pressure from your buyers about what work you show?
Yes, people have said things to me. "Why are you showing this horrible crap?" is for instance something they'll say if we're showing some really cutting edge stuff that they don't understand. And they say "where are the

beautiful more aesthetic pieces that you always show?" And I will say "well I don't always show that". Or I'll get the opposite. People who are buying really trendy photography say "why are you showing this boring painting that I wouldn't even want in my grandmothers house?" So they either trust me or they don't. I have collectors that would never buy his work *(points to Tom Leighton's piece)*. Ever.

But you don't let that affect what you show?
No I Can't. Can't. Because then that one collector could buy everything or he could buy nothing. But now if they became a backer then there might be an issue there that we would have to sort out. But then I have two arms – I have the Cynthia Corbett Gallery and corbettPROJECTS.

What's the difference?
corbettPROJECTS was formed when I was being offered all these offsite spaces in unusual places. When I formed that I went to the degree shows to find all the artists. Before that I was mainly showing artists who I had seen from galleries internationally.

In 2003 I was offered a little space in Liverpool Street and I did experimentation there for two years. I wanted to show really experimental art – like Performance art and Installation art. I set up corbettPROJECTS on this other arm, whereby if I never made money it wouldn't matter too much because I was getting most of it funded by beer sponsors. And it didn't cost me much to do. But then I was starting to get known and I was asked to apply to art fairs overseas like Arco and Artissima and that cost me money. So that's where it all started.

Do you think the art market can affect the work that artists are making today?
Yes of course. Of course it will. Because if you are an artist following the art market, particularly the young artists, you may be influenced by what is selling. And it depends how you are being taught as well because the art market is going to influence your teaching in the art colleges and then what's coming out is going to have an impact on the art market from the

teaching to the public. So yes I think there is no question. In Britain the YBA movement totally changed the face of the art that was coming out. A bit of a backlash is happening – well people say that but I don't think there was ever not painting and drawing in the YBA's.

Just like any field all great artists are affected and influenced by what came before them. Who wouldn't be? It's going to be the same thing in art. And I think what's so exciting is that there is so much more collaboration and mixing up of the art forms. And I think that the art market is going to embrace that. It looks like some of the artists who are coming out are not just visual artists but they might also be poets or musicians.

Are you less likely to sell the work to someone who appears to have a greater passion for investment and return rather than the art?
I'm a real democrat when it comes to art. The most recent example is Tom Leighton, some of his works were selling out and I was democratic about it. Whoever contacted me first got the work. In this case the person who contacted me first was a private client who actually hadn't collected that much and didn't have that much money. He got a photographic print that was just an addition – rather than the artist proof that was more expensive. There is no one that I wouldn't sell to.

Some people have said that if a collector came in wanting to buy all the artworks on show they would be worried in case that collector were going to sell it on right away – therefore decreasing the future value of the work. They are interested in profit – less so in the art.
I am not in that world yet. I have collectors and I think that is an issue. But I know that if someone was looking at all of her work *(points to the work of Yvonne de Rosa)* to buy we would have been thrilled, absolutely thrilled. And if they wanted to sell it all so be it.

I think it's when it's more of a commodity. I don't have any artists yet whose works are commodity-like. I would be so much happier if every time I had an exhibition big collectors, who would retain the works visibility, would buy. We are really excited when a museum buys from us or a big top collector or company. Anyone who is really a top collector is great because it means that the public will see it and there is more visibility.

Would you sell to me if I had lots of money?
I don't think you do have lots of money but it would be immaterial to me whether you did or didn't. And a lot of people who buy from me have very little money but they fall in love with pieces and they just buy it.

So you'd sell to anyone?
Oh yes. And I think that's one of the reasons why I have a very good reputation. People know that they can come to me and say "ok that's £21,000 I can't afford that, what can we do?" And usually I would try to give them a little bit of discount on my part if I can – if the artist allows me to. Then I will negotiate with you so you have a payment plan over the next three months, five months or whatever. I'd rather have someone who actually loves the piece buy it rather than someone who does not.

I bet you find it hard to let go of them after having them in your house?
I'm over that. There are obviously pieces here that are not for sale that the artist has given to me or I've bought. And they are pieces that would never be sold. Ever.

When collectors seek out art do they look to the reputation of a gallery first or do they look to the artist first?
The first thing that collector's do is look to the known galleries like White Cube, Lisson or Gagosian. It's normal. That's the way it is and as a young gallery who is not in that league you just have to be aware of that. The first port will always be "what are they showing?" And Victoria Miro; Timothy Taylor; Haunch of Venison. There will be galleries that have been going a very long time like Waddington's or Marlborough Fine Art and other galleries with a massive reputation because they have done so many great things for their artists and the art world. So if I was a collector, which I am a collector but not in that league, I would do the same. And when I

was studying contemporary art in the art history program I went to those galleries.

So my ambition is to be on that level of respect so the collectors will come to me like they go to them. But they will come to me for slightly different things i.e. young emerging artists.

The other thing that does happen though is that you get the random visit. But to get the random thing you have to be out there. You can't be just sitting, whether you are sitting here in Wimbledon or in Vyner Street. If the collectors do not go there they will not see you. That is why you do art fairs. A collector will wander by and they will look up and they will go "never heard of that gallery... but really interesting work". And go in. But they would never have come in otherwise. They would never have even seen it otherwise. And that has happened to me every time I'm in Miami, every time I'm in Chicago, every time I'm in New York. It's happened to me in Paris as well. Berlin it did not. I had wonderful people come but they did not make that connection and did not buy any of my artists.

So if I hadn't been and taken that risk I would not have met those collectors. I would not have met the journalists who saw the work. In Paris my main success there was that lots of journalists saw my work and went "well who is this gallery she's really intriguing?" "Who is she?" "What is she doing?" "Why does she have this amazing work?" and they kept leaving their cards. I just thought oh they're just being polite. Nope they emailed and called the next week. Tom Leighton ended up getting six pages in Le Monde.

So it's so much easier for collectors – who have no time – to go to a place where so many galleries are. Typically when I'm at fairs like Arco, which is so prestigious, one usually sees the back of someone amazing running by such as David Roberts or Frank Cohen. They are looking for the galleries that they know but they could just as easily see something else and go "wow amazing". And what I find is that if they don't buy there and then they will go home and if they were really taken by it they will go back to their office and Google me and Google the artist and they will do their research. So it's so important to have all that information on the website on the artist, the awards they've won and of work and future shows etcetera.

What for you makes a strong artwork?
Very different things. If someone were to analyse my taste it would be that it is eclectic! It would probably be quality in a sense that a lot of the work is quite technical. It's also to do with the dedication that someone has towards his or her art. I need to see that for me to really love the work. That really gets me involved and gets me interested. This guy for instance *(points to Tom Leighton's work)*, I'll take you around the house in a minute and show you his work, he will go to a city like New York and I would say "how did it go, how many photos did you take?" and he would say "oh thousands" and I would ask how many photos we were going to have for the next show and he would say 'maybe three'.

That's hard for me. But I know why it is and it's because he takes all those photographs and makes his artworks from them. And out of all of those he will tell me there are only three works of art in that. Or he will come back with just one photo after six months. And I have to just accept that. I know why that is – it's not because he's lazy or foolish, it's because he's good.

I love texture as well and layering. And the layers can be political, emotional or they can be physical. I love complicated layering in art works. The more complicated the better for me. I love the fact that when you see Kari Reis' work you look at it and you say "oh it's just so pretty, so glossy". But then when you know all what's behind it and the science and the pain she's gone through it's just amazing. Even if the artist is totally bonkers, mad, insane and crazy it doesn't matter, as long as they're serious about their art.

Are value judgments, monetary and critically a matter of subjective taste?
No it's not always subjective taste. You read the papers. Who's not going to buy Damien Hirst? Who in their right mind would not buy his work? He is the most successful artist. I mean I would have bought a print of his skull but I couldn't afford the £7,500 and I wasn't going to pay £1200 or whatever it was for an edition one of two thousand five hundred – I wasn't going to do that. It's subjective in the sense of why one person likes

something and another something else. Art is so personal, like music and theatre. But if someone powerful jumps on the band wagon and it becomes 'oh you should like this you should like that' and you get great reviews and loads of people like it human nature will make us think that if so many people like it then it must be good. And if you're an investor that's all that matters for you because if no one's going to like it no one's going to invest in it and you'll never be able to sell it for any return.

That's an investor I'm talking about. I'm not talking about an art lover. 'Art-collector-lover' vs. 'art-collector-investor' – although I do feel that you can be an 'art-collector-lover' and have a mind on investment. But you're never going to 'invest' in a piece of art if you think nobody is ever going to like it and it will never sell again. Because it's quite an objective, analytical thing and it has a methodology there and it's not unlike a lot of business.

I have had a few big collectors who ask me about investment value, "what do I think?" I just say that none of the artists that I represent have yet gone to an auction market like Sotheby's or Christie's. They've done private charity auctions but none have an official auction record. That's telling because once you have that then you have to make that all the time. You have to watch that. But all I can say is that when I saw Yvonne De Rosa in her degree show she was selling her work for £400 and now we sell her work for £900–£1500 for the same size. But that's probably what the price should have always been. Whereas, Tom Leighton's work has increased by about four hundred percent.

Do you think there are more 'art-investor-collectors' or more 'art-lover-collectors'?
Oh it's definitely more 'art-lover-collectors'.

That's good to hear
There are probably about two-hundred-and-fifty really serious art collectors in the world including companies, and about five hundred quite important collectors. And I'm not talking about museums, leave them

aside, museums are different; they will be driven a lot by art history, their collecting policy, the holes in their collection and their board.

Then there are about one thousand more and then there are just normal collectors. Then there are budding collectors. And some people act like collectors and start calling themselves collectors. A lot of my buyers will say "oh no I am not a collector just an art buyer". I will then say "it doesn't matter as an art buyer you are a collector".

When you go to other art galleries do you still get excited by the work that you see?
Yes of course.

Is art still rigorous or are we in an era of 'anything goes'?
I don't think anything goes. It must still be very rigorous because I think art is amazing wherever I go and it's phenomenal what I am seeing. But if you mean sloppy art there is a lot of sloppy art out there. But I don't pay much attention to sloppy art because it doesn't appeal to me. Even if that sloppy art ends up making millions, if it doesn't have that belief and that integrity and that commitment then I just don't have that interest in it.

Is it possible to spot themes or trends in Contemporary art? Is it possible to predict where art is going?
I don't know how to answer that question. I mean from an art historical point of view you see all the trends and you see where everything has been going has gone. I think that it's natural that artists will constantly want to push boundaries and be more creative and not derivative. To always do new things. Where is art going? I think as I was saying before with this collaboration. I think there is more freedom now. There's going to be more collaboration between different aesthetic fields and the lines won't be so stratified.

Who do you think the audience for art should be and who is your audience?
Anyone that's interested in art. People that love art are my audience. General public – well maybe they won't come here on a Sunday afternoon but

when I did the affordable art fair I must have met a thousand people in one day.

Why attend art fairs?
I am adamant that it's the most important thing. I don't even care what other gallerists say it's just such a democratic thing to go to art fairs as anyone can come in, anyone can be educated, anyone can ask questions. You can meet the most humble person and the top collector in the world, you never know. It's just a wonderful way to reach people and to expose your artists to a lot of people at the same time.

But all the art fairs are very expensive to do for the gallerist because you have to pay for it, you have to staff it, you have to get the work there, you have to print everything. It's very expensive. And you're running the risk that what you bring to the art fair no one will want to buy. But you at least get a reaction. And the art is there for everyone. And art fairs for me are the way that I get exposed into international contemporary art.

How do you decide whom to take to art fairs?
It's not about taking the best artists it's about taking the right artist for the exhibition at that time. It's like in Dublin it's a young market for Contemporary art so I can't take only really cutting edge stuff, but I'm taking quite a bit of cutting edge stuff because I'm not presenting my profile in a new country without showing who I really am. I could have taken all figurative and all painting but I'm not because that's not just what I do. So I'm taking a variety. And we'll see how it goes.

Do you think there is enough art criticism?
Yes. I think there's a lot of art criticism. We can hardly keep up with all the submissions for editorials we have to do. But I think it's varied; really conservative and parochial to really out there. I wish I could write more but I don't have time. I think people should maybe try to write about it if they're interested. And actually I think more artists, gallerists and art historians are getting involved with the critical art writing which I think is really good as

well and it's gone into the mainstream. And you can pick up any paper and you find articles on art, not just in the art pages. And it's really good that it's in the mainstream now. That's what I think. I don't know what anyone else thinks.

FURTHER RESOURCES

To find/submit additional learning resources
on the topic of the art market or 'professional
practice' please visit:

WWW.Q-ART.ORG.UK